Spirit
*
World

THE ESSENTIAL
MIND BODY AND SPIRIT BOOKS

Spirit ✳ World

Guides, ancestors, entities

Sirian Shadow

ROCKPOOL

A Rockpool book
PO Box 252
Summer Hill
NSW 2130
Australia

rockpoolpublishing.com
Follow us! rockpoolpublishing
Tag your images with #rockpoolpublishing

ISBN: 9781922468413

Published in 2026 by Rockpool Publishing

Design and typesetting by Sara Lindberg, Rockpool Publishing
Edited by Jessica Cox

Printed and bound in China
10 9 8 7 6 5 4 3 2 1

Contents

Introduction

Our world is alive with invisible energies. These subtle presences move around us, through us, and beyond us. Some people call them spirits. Others speak of guides, ancestors, or entities. Whatever the name, their existence transcends cultural boundaries and spiritual traditions, and they have played a powerful role in shaping human consciousness across time.

Spirit World is a deep dive into the unseen world: this book is designed to illuminate, contextualize, and demystify the wide range of spirits we may encounter on our paths. We will explore their histories and nature, and the many ways they have shown up throughout our existence. This book is for the seeker who wants to ground themselves in context before diving into practice.

Spiritual ecosystems are diverse and complex. In many traditions, spirits are not limited to the human dead, but include nature spirits, ancestors, animal spirits, and archetypal energies. Each tradition has its own lore, origin, and set of qualities. Understanding how people have recognized, revered, and interpreted these spirits throughout history provides a foundation for you to build a future relationship with them, if you choose to do so.

This book will also explore important frameworks, such as light and dark dualities, and the ethical responsibilities we hold as spiritual practitioners and curious observers. Whether you are new to this work or have years of experience, this book will help you better recognize the nature of spirit presence and give you an understanding of the vast terrain ahead. Above all, my intention is to offer an accessible, respectful, and balanced guide to the vast spiritual ecology that surrounds us.

The world of spirit is layered within this one, woven through the spaces between breath, emotion, and energy. Whether you've just sensed something beyond the veil or have experienced full moments of connection, chances are you want to understand more. This book is for seekers like you: those who know there is more to reality than what we can see and touch.

Spirit work is a deeply personal practice. While many teachings, frameworks, and traditions inform it, the most meaningful connection always comes from direct experience. This book is not a rigid system or dogma to follow, it's an invitation to explore the unseen, to develop your sensitivity, and to better understand the beings that move within the spirit world. As you move through these pages, remember that you don't need to follow someone else's path exactly. You're here to uncover what's true for you. Let your ancestors, your energy, and your intuition be your most honest compass.

You don't need to be a medium or psychic to start this work – you just need curiosity, a willingness to listen, and a commitment to self-awareness. This book offers foundational knowledge, historical context, and guidance to help you interpret, discern, and deepen your experience of the unseen world. It is your invitation to form a foundation of knowledge before developing your own relationship with the spirit world, which is grounded in personal experience and intuitive trust. You don't need to have all the answers before you begin. What matters is your willingness to notice, to listen, and to stay open.

In this book, we'll focus on understanding the landscape of the spirit world. Before we begin engaging in practice, we need to know where we are and who we're connecting with. This includes examining invisible energies, types of entities, historical frameworks, and the reasons people engage in spirit communication. In the chapters ahead, we'll build the foundational skill of sensing spiritual presence, an ability that often starts subtly but deepens with time, patience, and practice.

Sirian Shadow

PART 1

BECOMING FAMILIAR WITH THE SPIRIT REALM

CHAPTER 1

Invisible energies

We live in a world shaped not only by the tangible and the seen, but also by the subtle and the unseen. These invisible forces, what many spiritual traditions refer to as "energies," are present all around us, influencing our emotions, decisions, physical spaces, and even our relationships. While we might not be able to detect them with our five senses, their effects are deeply woven into the fabric of human experience. Whether understood through spiritual, mystical, or scientific frameworks, the presence of invisible energies is a foundational concept in spirit work you should understand before engaging with the spirit realm.

In ancient cultures, the belief in unseen forces was never questioned. The concept of "energy," in the metaphysical sense, predates modern physics and exists in nearly every cosmology, from the qi of Chinese medicine and philosophy to prana in Hindu traditions or mana in Polynesian spiritual systems. These early interpretations weren't just metaphors or superstitions, they were real, lived truths. To our ancestors, energy wasn't a fringe idea; it was a natural part of life that informed their understanding of healing, relationships, and the cosmic order.

Many Indigenous cultures understand the land itself as having energy, spirit, or consciousness. Mountains, rivers, trees, and rocks are beings with their own presence and wisdom. This belief fosters a sense of respect and reciprocity with nature, a sensitivity to the living spirit of the earth that creates a fertile ground for intuitive understanding and communication. When approached with reverence, the energies of nature can serve as guides, allies, and protectors in spirit work.

In modern times, with the development of quantum physics and exploration of energy fields in science, we are coming full circle – understanding that energy is not just a metaphysical concept, but a scientific one. Everything is composed of energy. At the quantum level, particles exist not as fixed points, but as probabilities and vibrations. Science confirms what mystics and shamans have said for centuries: that all matter is in motion, vibrating, resonating with frequency. Spirit work depends on being able to feel and engage with those frequencies.

But while science may support the existence of subtle energies, the language of spirit work is experiential and intuitive. This is the realm of the psychic, the empathic, the mystical. Spirit workers learn to "tune into" the unseen by quieting the noise of everyday thought and opening their intuitive senses. This is not a gift reserved for the select few; anyone can develop this skill with practice and patience.

How do we perceive invisible energy?

Invisible energy expresses itself through emotion, intention, presence, and connection. You've likely felt it already. The sudden chill in the room when someone enters with heavy emotions. The sensation of being watched when no one is there. The uplifting lightness when you're around someone joyful. Or the palpable heaviness that clings to a space after an argument. These aren't mere coincidences; they are energetic imprints.

You may already be more aware of energy than you realize. Ever walked into a room just after an argument and felt the tension hanging in the air?

Or noticed a loved one was upset before they said a single word? That's energy. It's the invisible residue of emotion, intention, or spiritual presence. Once you learn to recognize it consciously, spirit work becomes far more intuitive.

Not all energies are spirits. And not all spirits feel the same way energetically. Some are dense and heavy, others are subtle and soft, while some are electric or disorienting. Spirits carry their own frequency like a signature. Just as a friend's voice is immediately recognizable even if you're not looking at them, so too can spiritual energies eventually be felt and identified.

***

As spiritual practitioners, we learn to become sensitive to these energetic impressions. Every spirit, place, or person carries a frequency, a vibrational signature. Our job as spiritual practitioners is to develop the inner senses that help us attune to and understand those frequencies. Energy is the language of the spirit world. To communicate with spirits, interpret signs and messages, and form relationships with entities, we must first learn to sense and work with energy.

A fundamental principle in this work is that energy follows intention. Your focused thought, emotion, and will are tools through which you shape and direct energy. Spirits often respond more to intention than form. Rituals, candles, and incense are all powerful, but they are just vessels for intention. Without clarity of focus and sincere desire, a ritual is simply an empty performance. With intention, even the simplest gesture can become a profound invocation.

In many magical traditions, the concept of "raising energy" is central. Practitioners gather and build emotional and psychic energy to direct it toward a specific outcome. They can create this energy through chanting, dancing, breathwork, visualization, or emotional release. Once the energy is raised, intention shapes and directs it toward healing, protection, transformation, or communication.

The medium is the message

In spirit work, energy is the vehicle through which messages are transmitted. Divination tools such as tarot, pendulums, and scrying mirrors don't work simply because of their symbolism, but because of the energy channeled through them. When a spirit wants to communicate, they often impress their message energetically upon your subconscious, which you then interpret through the chosen tool or intuitive sense.

Energy is both the medium and the message. It is how spirits express themselves, and how we respond. It is the foundation for every interaction you will have in this realm. Whether you're offering healing to another person, creating a charm bag, invoking an ancestral guide, or cleansing a home, you are working with energy.

To truly understand spirits, therefore, you must first understand energy. It is not a vague or abstract concept, it is the breath of the world, the pulse of the unseen, the language of the soul. Most people associate energy with electricity or motion, but energy in spirit work is subtle, often intangible, and not easily measured. It's the energetic undercurrent of life itself, what some traditions call prana, qi, or life force. In truth, it doesn't matter what word you use. What matters is that you begin to develop a felt sense of it.

Everything that exists – bodies, thoughts, emotions, even spiritual presences – emits a kind of frequency. This isn't about pseudoscience or wishful thinking. Long before "energy" became a wellness buzzword, cultures worldwide already understood the nature of energetic resonance. Ancient healing systems like traditional Chinese medicine and Ayurveda are built entirely on an understanding of energetic flow. Mystics and shamans describe the sensation of feeling energy with their hands or perceiving it in visions. When someone says, "I got a weird vibe from that place," they're tuning into the same thing. Language may change, but the sensation is real.

Energetic imprints

Energy can imprint itself into places and objects. Houses can retain emotional residue from previous inhabitants. Antiques can carry the essence of their owners. Sacred spaces, temples, and altars become charged through repeated ritual use. Spirit workers may be called to cleanse or bless a space to reset its energetic field. Similarly, they use crystals and natural objects to amplify or transmute energy due to their vibrational properties.

Energy can also become distorted or blocked. Just as physical clutter affects a room, energetic clutter affects the spirit. Stagnant energy can lead to fatigue, irritability, or a feeling of being "off." This is why spiritual hygiene is so critical. Practices such as grounding, centering, shielding, and cleansing are essential. They help you maintain clarity, balance, and protection as you navigate different energetic landscapes.

In my own practice, I've encountered places where the air felt "thick," as if it were heavy with emotion. I've entered rooms where I instantly felt dread, grief, or anxiety, only to later discover that a traumatic event had occurred there. Conversely, I've been in sacred groves, temples, and homes where the energy was vibrant, joyful, and serene. These spaces feel alive with presence. Spirit workers become sensitive to these energetic cues, learning to read and interpret them with increasing accuracy.

YOUR AURA

Your own energy field is what many traditions call the aura. Your aura is your energetic body, which reflects your physical, emotional, and spiritual state. When you're grounded and in alignment, your aura expands, radiating outward with clarity and coherence. When you're stressed, sick, or emotionally drained, your aura can become contracted, fragmented, or permeable. A weakened energetic field can make you more susceptible to unwanted spirit influences.

Through meditation, breathwork, visualization, and intention, we can cleanse and strengthen our energy fields. We can also attune to the energy of spirits and others. Spirits may communicate by influencing our energetic field. A sudden shift in mood, a change in temperature, or a prickling sensation on the skin are all common signs that a spirit is near. But without energetic awareness, we may misinterpret or miss these messages.

Building your awareness

Along with benevolent energies are disruptive ones. Not all spirits or energies are kind or helpful. Some may be confused, lost, or malevolent. I don't mention this to instill fear, but to emphasize the importance of discernment. A vital part of a spirit worker's training is being able to distinguish between energies that are safe and those that are not. Your personal power, protection rituals, and spiritual boundaries are all important when working with spirits.

While you won't become an expert in energy overnight, you can start building your awareness. Just as we train our bodies for flexibility or strength, we can also train our subtle senses. Energy can be felt, moved, cleansed, and directed. This isn't as mystical as it sounds. It's part of being human; we're just not taught how to use it.

You don't need to be clairvoyant to start working with invisible energies. Most people expect some dramatic spiritual moment when they begin building awareness, but the first signs of energetic perception are often subtle: a physical sensation, a change in the air, or a gut feeling that won't go away.

HOW TO GET STARTED

Begin by paying attention. How do certain places make you feel? Do some spaces feel heavy, draining, or strangely quiet? Others may feel open, comforting, or gently buzzing with activity. The same is true for people. When you walk away from someone, if you feel like your energy has been pulled from you, you've picked up on an exchange that wasn't physical but energetic.

Part of developing awareness is energetic hygiene. We carry the residue of our environment and interactions with us until we intentionally release it. Think of it like spiritual dust. You might not see it but it accumulates over time. And just like a cluttered room can make it hard to focus, an energetically cluttered field makes it harder to hear or feel what's really present.

That's why regular grounding and clearing practices are vital tools to sharpen your sensitivity. There's no one right way to reset your energetic field. Simply drinking water, taking a salt bath, or walking in nature with the intention to clear yourself can do it. What matters is noticing how your energy feels before and after. Let experience be your teacher.

As your awareness sharpens, you'll begin to discern different energetic textures. A protective presence might feel warm and expansive. A distressed or restless energy might feel erratic or cold. Over time, you'll start to identify patterns. Just like learning to recognize flavors in food or tones in music, you train your discernment through exposure and attention.

Often, spiritual and emotional energies intertwine. An unresolved trauma may sit in the energetic field just as tangibly as a spiritual presence. Discerning the difference takes practice, but your body will usually know. Spirit work requires emotional honesty. If something makes you uneasy, don't override that feeling for the sake of curiosity. Respect your intuition, even if you don't yet have the words to explain it.

Subtle energies

We live in a culture that values logic and proof. But spirit work happens in the liminal spaces, where the languages spoken are sensation, intuition, and energy. You don't need to abandon critical thinking, but create room for your inner knowing to emerge.

Subtle energy isn't limited to ritual or meditation, it's everywhere. It's in the way you feel when you enter a crowded room, or when you sit beside someone whose inner world seems to pulse outward despite not speaking a word. Energetic sensitivity begins with spirit work, but it doesn't end there.

Many people unknowingly carry the energy of other people or places, or even emotional echoes from past experiences, clinging like static or settling like dust in our energy fields. One of the biggest turning points in my own development, when I felt something off, was learning to ask: "Is this mine?" This one question can reroute overwhelm into clarity. If something isn't yours, it can be released. If it is yours, now you know what to work with.

Some spirits, particularly guardians or guides, may help nudge your awareness when you've absorbed too much. This nudge could show up as a tension headache, a foggy mind, or a sudden mood dip. Developing inner awareness is part of learning to listen to their cues. Don't be afraid to ask for help clearing or regulating your field. That is also a form of connection.

SUMMARY

- » Energy is a core part of spirit work; it's present in all things and is sensed emotionally, physically, and intuitively.
- » Energy imprints places and objects; spiritual hygiene is key.
- » Developing sensitivity to energy is a learnable skill and subtle energetic awareness helps you perceive and communicate with spirits.

CHAPTER 2

Understanding different entities

Practitioners may encounter many kinds of spirits. Although this is not an exhaustive list, the following categories will help you differentiate their energies and decide if you want to connect with them. When you understand the different types of energies beforehand, you know what you may be dealing with and thus identify the kind of energy you would like to work with in your practice.

Land spirits

These are spirits who dwell within particular places or features of the land. They are connected to natural places, such as a certain river or specific mountain. Some of these spirits have achieved deity or godlike status; for example, the Hindu goddess Ganga is the goddess of the Ganges River. To begin working with land spirits, first identify sacred places in your area. These can be springs, crossroads, peaks, shores, and other thresholds. Next, spend time in and get familiar with the energy of these places. If you plan on leaving offerings, ensure they're environmentally friendly or, even better, clean a site of any litter.

Proper practice of working with land spirits includes asking them for permission to enter their domain. To do this, simply wait until you sense it's okay to proceed. Address them respectfully, introduce yourself, and listen. Pay attention to what rituals and offerings you intend to leave or create – be conscious of the land and that you aren't leaving anything harmful. You can always ask land spirits for guidance if you need clarity on offerings, but clean water is commonly accepted.

Spirits of place

When a spirit has imprinted on or is associated with a town or specific building, this can be a powerful place to meet them. The history of these spirits being venerated and revered spans worldwide. For example, household spirits or gnomes are found in many cultures like the *nisse* of Scandinavia, also known as *tomte*. In English and Scottish folklore, small, industrious spirits that inhabit houses and barns are called brownies. The word *húsvættir* (house wights), originates from Nordic culture and is a collective term for keepers of the household. To build a relationship with household spirits, begin by acknowledging and greeting them. Connecting with them can make for a peaceful and positive home environment. If you wish to give an offering, simply leave out a small portion of cream or milk, and keep the area comfortable and tidy. You can also use clean water as an offering.

Animal spirits

This term may refer to the archetype of an animal species or a singular animal spirit that manifests. Generally, they are benevolent spirits, which makes them much easier for beginners to work with. For example, in Norse mythology, *fylgjur* appear as animal attendant spirits that remain closely connected to the persona of their owners. Familiars are spirits that take the form of animals, aiding witches and cunning folk with their magical practice. Shamanic traditions include animal guides as protector spirits – you can meet your power animal through meditation and rituals like journeying or vision quests. The animal you connect with is often unexpected. If you are lucky enough to have met your power animal, research their characteristics and qualities to further understand the meanings and messages. The experience and discoveries can be incredibly fulfilling.

You may wish to honor your local animal spirits. Some practitioners place items connecting to the animal on their altar, such as feathers for those who connect with birds. Offerings will differ; pay attention to the animal spirit guide's characteristics to determine what would be appropriate. Clean water is also acceptable. A good rule of thumb is to ask for permission from your local spirits before taking anything in nature and intuitively wait for confirmation. It's considered polite to leave an offering in return. This does not need to be necessarily physical. The act of reducing your carbon footprint can be considered an offering.

Elementals

Also referred to as nature spirits, elementals are the life energy that runs through all living things and the elements of earth, air, water, and fire. Other traditions may include additional elements such as metal, wood, or ether depending on the cultural lens and cosmology through which the elemental forces are viewed. You can identify elemental spirits by their special association with some form or function within the earth's natural surroundings. Nature spirits or elementals don't have a one-size-fits-all explanation. Many Indigenous cultures believe spirits pervade all our existence and can be found in the land, water, air, and fire, as well as in all living things. Some traditions have crossovers between land spirits and elementals; however, elementals tend to be more primeval and are not sanctioned to a specific location.

Earth Spirits such as gnomes, fairies, leprechauns, and elves are all closely linked to the earth element. Earth spirits often embody qualities that help us engage with consciousness in a grounded, tangible way, bringing insight down to earth and into practical form.

Air Sylphs, or air spirits, can manipulate weather. They are present in the sky and are undetectable to the naked eye. Sylphs can detect even the tiniest changes in wind, humidity, temperature, or air pressure. They represent the air element through dancing, singing, performance, and artistic expression. The air element elicits positive emotions such as joy, contentment, amusement, and happiness. It serves as a reminder of life's joy and beauty. Art and music can freely flow into our life because of the quality of the air we breathe.

Water Nixies, naiads, ondines, undines, mermaids, and water nymphs are all names for water spirits. They are the embodiment of water's fluidity: nurturing, relaxing, releasing, receptivity, and beauty in nature. Although they are commonly shown as half-human, half-fish, they can take on any shape.

Fire Salamanders are associated with the element of fire. They are concerned with the intersection of passion, power, and knowledge. In the same way that fire is broad and active, salamanders also deal with motivating factors and a person's inner will. If someone has suppressed anger, the fire element can cause fury and a drive to control, as well as paranoia when their safety is endangered.

Once attuned to elemental energies, practitioners can often hear spirits through the earth, bodies of water, and in the wind. Adopting an animistic belief system, in which we view the world from a nonhuman point of view and ascribe life to everything, can assist us in connecting with these spirits.

Fairies

In folklore, fairies are beings who are strongly connected to the earth plane. Fairies generally serve and nurture the earth, including the plant and animal kingdoms. Ancient folklore depicts fairies as being once much more present and visible to humans, but now they hide themselves after humanity fell into greed and destruction and forgot their connection with the natural world. Fairies are described as spirits with humanlike attributes, magical abilities, and the power to shape-shift. They are depicted as having an inclination or natural tendency for tricks and mischief, although some praise their kindness and generosity.

With a fairy, essentially the energy you put out is what you will receive. According to folklore, fairies cannot tell lies, which makes them experts in deception or ambiguity. If you want to deal with fairies, you must have your wits about you. Approach working with fairies with caution. To remain in their good graces, you must follow a number of rules: keep out of trouble, never purposely disrespect them, and always be courteous. Many people believe it is impolite to say "thank you" or "I'm sorry" to fairies, because it diminishes their act of kindness. A better way to express your gratitude is to say something like "I express my gratitude or appreciation for …" or "You are most kind." You can apologize by saying, "My apologies," "Pardon me," or "I express regret." Offerings include honey and sweet, shiny, or natural gifts. Also, fairies regard reducing your carbon footprint and making an effort to help the environment as positive acts.

Ancestral spirits

Human relatives who have passed on become ancestral spirits. They may be your biological relations or those who had other connections to you, such as being part of your community or guardian spirits of your family. Paying tribute to or venerating ancestral spirits is a great way to begin spirit work because you usually already have a bond or connection with your ancestors. Because of their love and protection toward you, they will generally want to come to your aid. Keep in mind, spirit work with ancestors can be challenging if you don't know your lineage or history, or if you don't feel particularly close with them. If you want to work with your ancestral spirits, start by tracing your family roots and researching their history. Some practitioners create altars to honor them and use in their sacred space for their work. You can place your ancestor's favored items, food, or drink on the altar.

Angels

When most people think of angels, they adopt the widespread Christian ideas and concepts that they are winged humanlike beings who are God's messengers. In Islam, *malaikah* are believed to have been created before humans and communicate Allah's messages. Regardless of your religious beliefs, angels are incredibly powerful, divine spirits. The true nature of angels is debated because of their association with spirit guides. A guardian angel is another name for the spirits who are most commonly associated with spirit guides because of their loving disposition. For beginners, guardian angels are more supportive spirits to start working with.

Angels do not have a preference about where you draw your faith and beliefs from. According to John Dee and Edward Kelley's Enochian magic system, several hierarchies of angels, or intelligent rulers, are set over such things as the planets, the stars, and the four quarters of the earth. The *Arbatel de Magia Veterum*, an original sourcebook of angel magic, recognizes the existence of biblical angels, but also the pagan gods, entities who were subjugated to the Judeo-Christian God, thus being recast as angels and demons. These angelic entities are capable of both creation and destruction. Pre-Christian magi angels resemble something closer to a nightmare than the ethereal winged humanlike beings some people prefer to think of. Specificity is key if you wish to work with angels; they are divine beings of great power. Do your research to make sure you know exactly who or what you are contacting and working with. Offerings made to angels are commonly intangible; they are often energetic. Summoning and invoking them is lengthy and complicated – it's not for the beginner.

Demons

These entities are typically associated with evilness and malevolent behaviors or characteristics. Western culture often characterizes demons through the lens of Christian theology or other Abrahamic traditions, but demons appear across many world religions, such as Hinduism and Zoroastrianism. Demons aren't entirely different from angels – neither demons nor angels have ever been human, so they don't understand or relate to what it is to be human. They are not concerned with making your path easier, and both can be destructive in bringing you what you want. Throughout history, demons are considered to be opposers and masters of defiance. The truth is that demons have their own agenda. Working with them can be ambiguous – it's not for beginners. If you are able to understand a demon's motives and can align them for your own benefit, or learn how to control them, they can make for powerful allies. You can also call on angels and demons for protection. To banish them, methods include sulfur and blessed water. Working with demons is most commonly found in the Goetia tradition. For Solomonic magicians, demons can make great employees; however, for those who aren't adept at such workings, they can be the worst bosses.

Deities

Simply put, deities are divine or sacred spirits. They are incredibly powerful and vary among different cultures, each with their own myths, traits, and moralities. In polytheistic religions, deities are worshipped as gods or goddesses. In monotheistic religions like Christianity, deities are the supreme being, creator, and authority of faith.

Working with them can be a rewarding experience and an opportunity to acknowledge the divine in a personified manner. For anyone wanting to develop a relationship with deities, start by researching what interests you. Are you drawn to ancient Greek myths? Or Egyptian gods and goddesses? Choose what you feel compelled to study and learn about, then use that knowledge as the foundation to build your practice.

During your studies, you'll discover what offerings are acceptable for certain deities. Clean and fresh water is almost universally accepted. I've found it beneficial to charge the water with the ruling planetary alignment associated with a patron. For instance, Athena's ruling planet is the moon, so water charged under moonlight is a perfectly acceptable offering. Although each relationship varies, the common denominator for remaining in their good graces is to treat deities with the utmost respect.

A lot of new devotees will try to dive right into deity work; however, many don't understand the long journey and commitment it takes to form a relationship. If working with deities interests you, first form relationships with your ancestors and local land spirits. This is a great way to build a foundation and realize their existence relates and connects to other spirits.

Cosmic beings

Also known as extraterrestrials and extradimensional beings, cosmic beings are from other planets and often exist in a different dimension from ours. Some beings are considered so far advanced that they can travel across dimensions, time, and space. In new age beliefs, starseeds, or star people, are traveling souls with cosmic-being lineage, who have incarnated on earth to inspire and heal humankind. Just as the species of cosmic beings vary, so do their motives and intent. Some incarnate to help humans evolve, while others seek to support a darker mission – not all these souls intend love and light. Our knowledge of starseeds and cosmic beings come to us through channelers. One indicator that you may be a starseed is feeling a longing for home and having a sense that earth is not where you originated from; the human experience may feel foreign to you.

SUMMARY

- Spirits come in many forms, such as land spirits, ancestors, animals, and deities.
- Understanding their traits helps you engage with them respectfully and intentionally.
- Research, offerings, consent, and discernment are key in building spirit relationships.

CHAPTER 3

Energetic allies and identifying spirits

Spirit guides are not wish-fulfillment fantasies or invisible babysitters. They're not here to take control of your life, and they're not obliged to show up just because you've called. These relationships are sacred. Like any meaningful relationship, they require reciprocity, clarity, and patience. There's a tendency, especially in new age spaces, to romanticize spirit guides as ever-present beings dispensing cosmic wisdom on command. In reality, they are complex, distinct intelligences, each working with us in unique ways depending on our capacity, path, and willingness to engage with respect.

The word "guide" itself can be misleading. It implies these beings are somehow above you, or that you're supposed to follow their advice without question. But your guides are not infallible. They don't live your life, walk your path, or bear the consequences of your choices. You do. They can see from a wider vantage, but they shouldn't override your will or evolution.

Spirit guides don't exist to boost your ego or inflate your spiritual résumé. Their role is to support your growth, sometimes through encouragement, other times through challenge. A guide won't hand you answers. They'll invite you to grow into them. If you're leaning too heavily on them, they may withdraw and wait until you've done your own inner work before offering guidance again. This isn't punishment, it's respect. A good guide wants you to become sovereign, not dependent.

GUIDES OF ALL KINDS

Spirit guides can take many forms. Some people connect with ancestors, known or unknown, who continue to walk with their lineage. Others experience animal spirits, elemental beings, or star energies. Some are accompanied by teachers from past lives, ascended masters, or cultural archetypes. It's not uncommon to have guides whose identities remain mysterious for long periods of time, communicating only through sensation, dream, or symbolic language.

One of the early challenges in building these relationships is trying too hard to define them. We want names, roles, lineages – something to make it all feel "real." But spirit communication isn't always tidy. A being may show up as a symbol – such as an animal, a recurring number, or a shape seen in dreams or visions – before it ever speaks. It may be felt as a presence before it takes on a visual form. The connection unfolds over time, and just like in the physical world, forcing clarity too early can damage trust.

Another challenge is projection. If we carry unresolved dynamics with authority figures, parents, teachers, or religious leaders, we may unconsciously cast those patterns onto our guides. We might hear harshness when spirits are silent or assume disapproval when they're only waiting. Ask yourself: Is this message truly coming from spirit, or is it echoing something from my own psyche? The more you refine your inner landscape, the more clearly you'll discern true connection from imagination or fear.

Finding your guides

Learning to recognize the presence of your guides is less about flashy spiritual theatrics and more about cultivating subtle awareness. You may receive a quiet nudge, a recurring symbol, a dream that lingers, a sudden knowing that arrives without logic. Sometimes, it's the feeling that someone is with you when you're otherwise alone, or a gentle energetic shift when you ask for support. These small moments are invitations. If you're waiting for a full apparition in robes with a booming voice, you may miss the real conversation that's already happening.

While ritual can help you build consistency in this relationship, the ritual itself isn't the source of connection, you are. Spirit guides respond to presence, sincerity, and clarity. Whether you light a candle, say a prayer, or sit quietly with intention, what matters most is that you're showing up in a way that honors the energy you're inviting in. Be honest. Be respectful. Don't demand. Instead, offer. Offer your attention, your gratitude, your curiosity.

OPEN CHANNELS OF COMMUNICATION

One effective way to open communication is to create a dedicated space in your home. It doesn't have to be elaborate, just a shelf with a white cloth, a small bowl of water, a candle, and a few personal items is enough. What matters is the energy with which you tend to it. You're not "worshipping" your guides, you're simply creating a point of access, a frequency they can recognize. Over time, this space becomes an anchor. Just entering it can shift your state of consciousness, making it easier to listen.

Journaling is another method. Write down your experiences, even if they seem minor or uncertain. A sudden temperature change, a phrase that pops into your head, a dream that woke you – these moments add up. Over time, you'll notice patterns. Certain symbols may repeat themselves. Particular feelings may accompany their presence. You find that what felt random or disconnected at the time reveals itself in hindsight to have been guided all along.

It's important to learn to differentiate between intuition and fear. Spirit rarely speaks in anxiety. If a message feels frantic, paranoid, or rooted in urgency, it's probably coming from your own nervous system, not your guides. Real guidance tends to be calm and steady, even when it's challenging. It may arrive as a whisper, but it carries weight. It sticks with you.

Trust is everything in spirit work. But trust isn't built overnight. It comes from consistency, from testing the waters, from discerning what's true and what's projection. And it's okay to question your guides. They'd rather you ask for clarity than follow in confusion. This is a partnership, not a dictatorship. Ask them for signs, not to test them, but to practice communication. Pay attention to and keep track of what unfolds. Let the relationship reveal itself gradually, like an image coming into focus.

The form our guides take often reflects what we're ready to perceive. Some appear as ancestors, familiar energies with deep roots in our bloodlines. Others may sense animal spirits, elemental beings, or otherworldly guides. These forms are less about literal identity and more about symbolic resonance. A wolf guide may represent loyalty, protection, and instinct, or it may reflect a connection to the wildness you've lost touch with. A grandmother figure may show up not because she was your biological relative, but because you need the comfort, wisdom, or grounding that this archetype provides.

Your guides may change over time

As we grow, so do our needs, and different spirits may step forward depending on the phase we're in. Some guides will walk with you for a lifetime. Others come for a single lesson or moment. There's no hierarchy, no scarcity. You're not "losing" a guide if their presence becomes quieter, you're evolving. And they are too. Spirit allies are not stagnant. They're alive in their own right, with their own journeys and roles to fulfill.

In spiritual spaces, we tend to create rigid frameworks around guides: this one is "higher," that one is "lower," this one is "yours forever," or you must have a certain number of guides. But relationships with spirit don't work like a corporate organization chart. They're fluid, personal, and dynamic. Trying to force them into a structure can limit your connection rather than deepen it.

Instead, remain open and allow for surprise. A guide might show up in song lyrics, the flicker of a candle, or a phrase repeated by three strangers in a single day. These synchronicities aren't accidents, they're spirit's language. It's subtle but precise. Once you start noticing it, it becomes impossible to ignore. And yes, sometimes you'll get it wrong. You'll misread a signal, mistake your own desire for direction, or go through dry spells when it feels like no one's listening. That's part of the path. It doesn't mean you're disconnected or broken, but that you're learning how to attune. Just like any relationship, it takes time, effort, and humility. But the rewards are immense.

Having a relationship with spirit guides isn't about giving away your power, it's about remembering you were never alone. These allies are here to support your sovereignty, amplify your intuition, and walk beside you as you navigate the beautiful mess of being human. As your connection deepens, it often becomes less about asking for signs or answers and more about listening for presence and moving in alignment with trust. That's the real gift: not just having guides but becoming a guide to yourself.

Some good indicators that a spirit is close by include:

- constantly hearing their name
- being unable to stop thinking about them
- having impeding thoughts or images linking to them
- feeling drawn to wanting to discover more.

Stronger relationships with spirits can be formed in similar ways to human friendships. When you establish common ground and similar interests, or share mutual admiration and traits, you feel inclined to connect with them and vice versa.

Where to meet your guides

You can't always meet spirits in the comfort of your sacred space. If you seek to connect with a particular archetype, you may need to visit them in a neutral setting where they like to gather. If you're seeking an engagement with spirits and aren't ready to invite them into your space, then perhaps visit them at crossroads and thresholds. These natural intersections and convergences of energy are active places for meeting spirits.

Thresholds and crossroads are places that emit the intense and powerful energies spirits crave. Their presence in these places adds to the magnitude of energy. While crossroads maintain a point of intersection, thresholds hold the space of bordering elements or energies. For instance, a shoreline where the land meets the sea is a threshold. Cemeteries and delivery rooms are considered thresholds of life and death.

Other places of connection with spirits include their shrines and temples. Shrines and temples can be natural or human-made. Natural shrines may develop in a water spring or tree, with the portal opening because of the intense concentration and continued patronage of devotees. Energy follows thoughts. Spirits may come forward when you give them attention and intense focus. Acts of reverence often generate spirit interactions. You may please a spirit by providing a home for them, such as planting a tree or building an altar.

ASTRAL ENCOUNTER

Meeting my spirit guide for the first time on the astral plane was a profound experience. After setting the intention of meeting my spirit guide and following a guided meditation, she appeared to me as a tall, blue-skinned alien. She was bald except for a tiara-like band across her forehead. Although humanlike, she was very slender with elongated extremities. I don't remember her speaking, all I could feel was immense love emanating from her. Her energy was maternal and compassionate. I felt a clear feminine energy coming from her. At the time, I had very little information about alien spirits, which I refer to as star or cosmic beings. One day, I was scrolling online and came across a picture of a bald, blue-skinned alien with pointy ears that stopped me in my tracks. It was the closest artistic depiction I'd seen of my spirit guide, and confirmed my belief in our capability to spiritually connect with beings who are not human.

Working with deities

Although my experience with my guide was very positive, you don't want to rush into working with powerful entities such as deities until you understand how spirits appear and communicate. Visions, messages, and communication with spirits and deities are most commonly experienced on the astral plane and in deep meditative states. You should only attempt to reach deities after you become familiar with working and channeling human energies or spirit guides. Like angels and demons, deities are incredibly powerful energies, devoid of human traits and emotions. They do not think or act like us, and certainly do not look like us. Spirit guides and ancestors are much more forgiving because they generally care about us and communicate in more familiar ways.

Humans gave deities personified traits to help people connect with and establish a more rational relationship with them. We put a face to the energy so people may fear them less and simplify devotional acts like paying tribute.

I have a cautionary tale about working with deities. After I had spent some time working with and venerating my matron deity, she appeared to me on the astral when I was in a deep meditation. For me, visiting the astral realm is like a lucid dream. I am conscious of my surroundings and in command of my actions. However, in this instance there were no surroundings, only a dark abyss. A massive green snake emerged out of the void, not slithering on the ground but standing upright and towering above me. If you like snakes, this experience may not have been frightening for you; however, I was frozen in fear.

When the snake leaned forward toward me, I decided to demonstrate my bravery, that I was not terrified of its appearance. I extended my hand in an attempt to pat the snake. This was a tremendous error.

Assume you're traveling somewhere you don't speak the language. What methods do you use to communicate with the locals? You probably use gestures and point to symbols, signs, and other items, as well as use motions and body language. The same is true if a spirit appears to you and speaks in a language other than your native speech. Pay attention to their body language and any other methods of communication they use. Deities frequently appear in the shape of creatures with whom they are linked, and they rarely talk when in animal form.

The snake was my matron, who bowed forward as a greeting. Misunderstanding, I impolitely and ignorantly tried to pat her head, when a courteous bow would have been the appropriate response as a sign of respect and greeting.

Up until then, in exchange for my devotion, she had granted any desire I petitioned her, as long as my intention was aligned with hers. For example, I once petitioned her for help to increase the number of my supporters and patrons so I could widely share my work and artistry to provide genuine value, support, and help to others. Shortly afterward that number grew exponentially.

After our interaction on the astral plane, however, she did not fulfill my petitions. No matter what I asked my matron for, and no matter how great the offering, it either did not come to fruition or came with bad karma. All I could do was humbly ask for forgiveness to reclaim her grace and love. Apologizing and asking for forgiveness usually includes an offering. Sometimes a spirit may forgive a devotee and reconnect with them, and sometimes the damage has already been done so it will not.

How did I know the entity was my matron when she appeared as a snake and didn't speak? Apart from my claircognizant ability and inner knowledge, I later learned that snakes are one of her sacred creatures. My intuition informed me she wasn't an animal spirit because of her massive size and manner. I also hadn't established the intention or called on any animal spirits beforehand. Everything pointed to my matron, from the signs and timing to the work and intentions I had established. Because I had conducted considerable study before forming a connection with her, I could recognize her when she appeared.

HOW TO IDENTIFY SPIRITS

When you meet a spirit, to help you identify them, pay attention to your actions and intentions beforehand, who you are consciously or purposefully asking to connect with, and what you have asked the universe for. You can accurately identify using a combination of common sense, critical thinking, research, intuition, and the process of elimination. Spirits may not meet us on the astral plane, but they may visit us in different ways such as in dreams or providing synchronicities.

Begin by considering who the spirit could be, determining what characteristics you perceive, then eliminate those spirits with dissimilar characteristics. When in doubt, use divination or ask for signs of confirmation. Lean into the feeling of knowing by trusting your instincts. Spirits often send us signs or symbols to confirm their identity.

SUMMARY

» Spirit guides are not all-powerful beings; relationships require trust and reciprocity.

» Communication is often symbolic or intuitive, not always verbal or visual.

» Journaling, signs, and consistent practice help identify and strengthen your connections.

» You need caution and discernment when working with deities and unfamiliar spirits.

CHAPTER 4

Light and dark

People have unfounded fears and beliefs about spirit work and whether or not it's "evil." The concept of evil is a human construct. We are part of a world containing both positive and negative entities, energies, and events. Unfortunately, some people use misinformation to project fear about spirit work. When a powerful organization tells you to fear something, ask yourself why. We must pull back the curtain to discover the root of that fear. Once you dive deeper, you'll realize that many fears have been projected onto us with ulterior motives. We think the fear is to keep us safe, when in actuality it's to govern control and maintain power. Exercise due diligence with research and cross-checking of credible resources. The information in this book should not be used to control or restrict your beliefs, but empower you to use critical thinking and discern what you believe to ease any apprehension, doubts, or anxiety toward spiritualism.

Spirit work can absolutely benefit its practitioners. For the determined, brave, and investigative practitioner, it can give you a greater understanding of universal truths, and when applied appropriately it can bring improved health, prosperity, and wisdom.

We can all make a conscious choice to connect with light or dark energies – both exist simultaneously. Spirit work is a metaphysical practice that can create change in our physical reality. The work itself is a spiritual and sacred art form. Practitioners can tap into the source of power – an unbiased and neutral natural energy – then use it as intended. So, in terms of the work being good or evil, it is neither until a practitioner utilizes this natural force. The intention of the practitioner creates the label – creative or destructive, help or harm – not the work or energies themselves.

We use many metaphors to categorize the meaning of entities like demon or angel. Energies are not only black and white; this categorization warps the understanding of energy and spiritualism. An energy's nature cannot be categorized as easily as light or dark, good or evil, high or low. It is neither because it is both, existing as one. Energy has both positive and negative charges; likewise in energetic terms, spirits, entities, beings, angels, and demons are both.

Therefore, spirit work has nothing to do with evil, and most practitioners don't even work with the idea of evil at all. Anyone with an interest in working with darker spirits should already understand that the work cannot be categorized or labeled as such. Varied forms of the work, including witchcraft, never actually include such energies or destructive forces. Although some practitioners choose to work with demons, who's to say the intention of their work is "evil?" Only the practitioner knows that. Even though some practitioners may choose to work with these forces in their practice, fears often arise from misunderstanding.

Spiritualism was never categorized or associated with being "evil" until the emergence of modern media and inventions like radio and television. Before these inventions, spiritualism was viewed as a positive practice. Mediumship, channeling messages, and communicating with spirits were about relaying messages of hope and providing closure for peace and love. However, the narrative about spirits altered with the dawn of mass entertainment. Some people enjoy the adrenaline rush of being scared. But for the gullible and weak-minded, the rise of entertainment blurred the line between fact and fiction.

Two sides to every energy

Every energy you work with – whether it's a spirit, deity, angel, or demon – has light and dark sides. The work is neither good nor evil; your intention specifies its purpose. When we refer to spirits as angels or demons, this is a metaphor that doesn't depict their true energetic nature in a practical sense.

Effective spiritual workers or practitioners need to be open to meanings or definitions that span all cultures and associated languages. We must understand the importance of our intention and associations through language, not the word itself. The meaning of a word can vary and be redefined to fit a person's beliefs more accurately based on many variables.

My wish for you is to have the freedom to develop your own beliefs, which you generate yourself from what you discern and understand, using your own critical thinking to decipher information and your experiences. No one can choose your moral compass and ethical code for you. Although most people do abide by universal ethics, your individual perception and experience will help give the clarity you need to move forward in spirit work. Believing something simply because someone told you will not give you the results you desire, and it will leave you constantly second-guessing your instincts and intuition. Learning how to use your own discernment and tune into your feelings from your personal experiences, however, will give more powerful results.

Entities should not be constrained into simplistic black and white, or light and dark categories. They are more nuanced. Dark deities like Lilith and Lucifer, for example, are feared because of their demonic associations, but are also venerated for their protective qualities. If you remove the literary context, their energy is both, just how people are capable of portraying both qualities.

Working with dark energies

Whether they are of the light or dark, working with spirits comes down to your intention behind initiating a relationship. If your goal is to evoke the embodiment of evil, then it will more than likely bring about nothing more than some spiritual anarchy or chaos. At the very worst, it may cause some actual harm. But if your goal is to discover the mysteries of hidden knowledge, defy social structure, or harness and experience healing powers, the experience can be a positive one, even if the entity you petition is referred to as the "Devil."

The "Devil" of ancient folklore has very different behaviors and traits from the Christian Satan. Practitioners working in this space find it useful to think of them as different entities; not all demonic practices are satanic. From my research, most Satanists don't work with demons at all. The author of *The Satanic Bible*, Anton LaVey, was an atheist. The Church of Satan is an atheist institution that views the existence of the Christian God and Devil as insufficient, mistaken, or outweighed by arguments and evidence indicating there isn't reason to believe in their existence.

Atheistic Satanists have absolutely no interest in worshipping the Devil and regard Satan as a symbol better characterized by the humanistic traits that Christians demonize, such as pride, liberalism, and individualism. Satanic magic does not involve working with demons, and although Satanists may use a symbol for Satan in rituals, they don't actually worship a divinity. People who work with demons, more than utilizing symbols in rituals, are rarely practicing satanic magic, and magical workings with demons seldom have anything to do with Satanism, paganism, or religion.

Some historical records describe witches who have worked with demons or the Devil with the intent of harming and hurting others, but these are often, if not all, fabricated cases from their accusers during the witch-hunt era in North America and Europe. In these cases, the accused were not working with Satan, performing black masses, devil worship, or any such practices. The only "evil" came from the actions of those who murdered innocent people – whether they were accusers, bystanders, or executioners – who took someone's life or tortured them against their will. They are the true faces of evil.

Ceremonial magic

In witchcraft and folk magic, working with demons is highly uncommon. In Goetic and ceremonial magic, however, there are records of calling and working with demons.

Ceremonial magic incorporates a wide variety of long, elaborate, and often complicated rituals. The most prominent practitioners of ceremonial magic include Aleister Crowley and John Dee, who are for many people synonymous with it. A key element to performing ceremonial magic is the invocation and evocation of entities, both angels and demons, from Jewish and Christian lore.

Categories of ceremonial magic include Enochian and Goetic. Enochian magic comes from the recordings of John Dee and Edward Kelley, who were said to receive their knowledge directly from angels. Goetia is the term for a type of magic that conjures or summons spirits, especially demons. Ceremonial magic is challenging, to say the least, and requires a lot of study because of its complexity. It is demanding and not suitable for the beginner practitioner. The goal of Goetic magic depends on the practitioner's intent and which demon or entity they summon; their intent can include anything from curing illness to gaining wealth, while the summoned entities' motives and moods can vary from obsequious and dutiful to untamed and defiant. Practitioners would be wise to remember the most important rule of conjuration: never summon what you cannot banish!

THE IMPORTANCE OF CROSSROADS

Stories of people making deals with demons or the Devil at a crossroad are common in folklore, and the crossroad spirit is much older than Christian belief. Crossroad spirits often go by other names and, depending on your beliefs, these spirits are not malevolent at all. They can be fiercely protective and loving toward their devotees. In Greek mythology, crossroads are associated with both Hermes and Hecate. In the Vodou tradition, Papa Legba is the *lwa* of crossroads and a messenger to the spirit world. When working with spirits, you should identify who you are working with and not just let labels or another's beliefs dictate who that entity is.

In my experience, it's much easier to form a relationship with a deity or spirit with personified traits rather than an abstract divine force. Aside from forming spiritually fulfilling relationships, entities in any context can be powerful allies. But very few entities are 100 percent good or bad. Just like people, spirits and deities have strengths and weaknesses. Even the Abrahamic God has flaws, and if you don't believe me, you may need to revisit the Old Testament. The point is, you already know how to assess the risks associated with people, so apply the same discernment you would use for human relationships to the spiritual kind.

Demons

The concept of demons is much older than what most people would consider. Demons are often associated as dark or malevolent forces and entities, but after my research I regard them as often rebellious and independent, although intensely powerful beings. Popular belief associates them with Abrahamic religions, but demons date back to ancient religions and philosophy. Therefore, a practitioner working with demons does not mean they are working with Abrahamic and Semitic religions.

Even the etymology of the word "demon" highlights inaccuracies with them being evil. The word "demon" originates from the ancient Greek *daimon*, which means a "lesser god or divine power". In this sense, a demon is a protector, guardian, or patron spirit. The association with malevolence didn't appear until the rise of Christianity, when it was used in a Latin version of the Bible authorized and used by the Roman Catholic Church. As Abrahamic and Semitic religions spread, Western cultures adopted a definition of demons being unclean or evil spirits associated with heathens. In psychology, however, the daimonic refers to a natural human impulse to affirm, assert, perpetuate, and increase the self to its totality. As you can see, the literary sense of "demon" is very different from the true nature of a spirit.

Another example of the nature of a spirit versus its literary metaphor appears in the book series His Dark Materials by Phillip Pullman. In this series, Pullman uses the Latin spelling "dæmon" for a being that is the outer physical manifestation of a person's inner self, which takes the form of an animal. Along with the spelling, Pullman uses the word's Latin definition, describing dæmons as an aspect of his characters' human nature, which is not associated with evilness. Each character's dæmon has its own character, which is connected to their counterparts and in relation to their conscience and internal voice. Dæmons appear in the opposite gender to their connected characters, establishing a balance of their character's true nature – like an outward and visible representation of a balance between yin and yang, or divine feminine and masculine energies.

The duality and unity of paradoxes is central to the yin–yang philosophy, which suggests that the universe is designed to have balance. Everything is both yin and yang, and both sides can exhibit dominant characteristics. It is important to seek the light within the dark and recognize the darkness within the light. This idea is at the heart of Tao. It is a dynamic construct – not static but constantly blending and balancing. For us to become truly whole, we must embrace both the dark and the light.

Far too often, we try to neatly package and label things. My example of how Western civilizations mostly relate the word "demon" to its contemporary and religious context, rather than its historical meaning or the nature of the being, demonstrates that beliefs are skewed by language. But imagine now that a demon is capable of both creation and destruction, harm and help. So if a demon is capable of much more than malice, why can't angels be capable of more than good?

High and low magic

To the naive and uneducated, high magic may depict a heavenly practice and low magic an infernal one. But in truth, high and low magic simply differ in their application and appeal to different personalities and tastes. They can be categorized as follows:

- Low magic is nature-based.
- High magic is ceremonial or ritualistic.

High magic should not be used for bringing about earthly pleasures and physical manifestations. Its goal is to gain knowledge and is focused on an "initiation" that marks a union or transition from being mostly unconscious to mostly conscious. Neither form of magic is associated with evilness or goodness; both are neutral until a practitioner attaches intent.

For example, think of a pencil. You can use a pencil as a tool for beneficial purposes or harmful purposes; its intent relies on the person wielding the tool. The same rings true for the work. Remember, the moon reflects the light of the sun as it crosses the night's darkness. As the sun illuminates all things, it also casts shadows on what it touches. There is good in every evil and evil in every good. Everything related to a function or position has its own intrinsic value.

SUMMARY

Should your practice include working with light or dark, angels or demons? It comes down to your intent. Do you mean to help or harm? Are you working for a person's greatest good, or seeking to have control over them? How you perform the work is a matter of choice.

» Spirit work is neutral; your intention defines whether it's constructive or harmful.

» Cultural fear of "dark" spirits often stems from media and institutional control.

» Personal beliefs about spirits warrant thoughtful reflection, especially when it comes to darker energies, which often demand a deeper understanding.

» Spirits can be complex and not strictly good or evil.

CHAPTER 5

Inner sight and psychic senses

There's more to reality than what is visible to the physical eye. Across time and cultures, seers, diviners, oracles, and visionaries have moved between worlds, reading the currents of energy, spirit, and fate. What we now commonly refer to as "psychic senses" were once understood as sacred gifts, essential to the community's health and guidance. Though the vocabulary has changed over time, the phenomena themselves remain strikingly consistent.

Psychic perception is rarely confined to one sense alone. Rather, it unfolds through a wide spectrum of subtle impressions, collectively known as the "clairs":

- **Clairvoyance** The ability to see with the mind's eye, or "inner sight."
- **Clairaudience** Hearing sounds no one else can hear.
- **Clairsentience and clairempathy** Feeling sensations or emotions that do not originate from one's own experience.
- **Claircognizance** Knowing something without logical reasoning.

- **Clairalience** Smelling scents that carry spiritual significance.

References to these faculties appear in spiritual texts, oral traditions, and folk practices worldwide. In ancient Greece, the Oracle of Delphi received messages, visions, and impressions from the god Apollo in a trance state. In many Indigenous cultures, medicine people or shamans have long served as bridges between the visible and invisible realms, receiving messages from ancestors, spirits, or nature itself. Medieval Christian mystics described ecstatic states where they heard the voice of God or saw visions of angels and saints. And in the nineteenth and early twentieth centuries, the Spiritualist movement ushered in a renewed public fascination with mediumship, séances, and "second sight."

This resurgence of interest in psychic phenomena in the West was not just spiritual but also cultural. In a time of rapid industrialization and scientific progress, people hungered for mystery, desired to reclaim what had been lost in the cold rationalism of modern life. Psychic abilities, once relegated to myth and mysticism, became the subject of study and experimentation. Organizations like the Society for Psychical Research emerged to catalog and investigate unexplained experiences. Prominent figures, including writers, scholars, and even scientists, openly engaged in séances and extrasensory perception (ESP) testing, lending credibility to what had long been dismissed as superstition.

The distinction between psychic and mediumistic abilities also began to crystallize during this period. While both involve ESP, they operate differently. Psychics receive impressions through their own energetic fields, reading the emotions, thoughts, and future potentials of people, places, or objects. Mediums serve as a conduit for communication with spirits, acting as a bridge for entities, often departed loved ones or guides, who wish to relay messages from the other side. Many individuals exhibit both abilities.

Spirits interact with the world of the living in subtle but perceptible ways. The methods and mechanics of these interactions are complex, with various cultures offering different interpretations. In some traditions, spirits influence dreams, appearing with messages, warnings, or blessings. In others, they manipulate the physical environment, such as flickering candles, cold drafts, untraceable whispers, or the sudden scent of something familiar. In times of grief, many report sensing the presence of a loved one who has passed, a weight on the bed, a voice in the dark, or an overwhelming feeling of peace.

A long history

Accounts of spectral interaction go back millennia. Ancient Mesopotamians conducted detailed rituals to honor and appease the dead, out of both reverence and fear. The ancient Romans practiced Lemuralia, a festival to exorcise restless spirits. In African diasporic traditions, the spirit world is as real and close as the physical, with one's ancestors not gone but transitioned, watching and guiding from beyond. And in East Asian cultures, ancestral veneration remains a cornerstone of spiritual life, and dreams, symbols, and signs are common forms of spirit communication.

Even today, in a world dominated by technology and empirical thinking, people frequently report psychic impressions and spirit contact. They are often shared in hushed tones, not because they're rare, but because they are deeply personal. Most people, if answering honestly, have had at least one experience they couldn't explain: a dream that came true, a premonition that saved them, a gut feeling they didn't ignore and were later grateful for. These moments speak to something enduring, an ancient thread of perception that exists within us all, even if dimmed by skepticism or cultural conditioning.

Though psychic sensitivity exists on a spectrum, nearly everyone has the capacity to perceive beyond the five physical senses. The difference in ability is often awareness, trust, and conditioning. Many young children report seeing lights, sensing invisible presences, or knowing things they haven't been told. Well-meaning adults may dismiss, minimize, or even punish these perceptions, in wanting to protect children from ridicule or fear. Over time, the child learns to shut down these perceptions, relegating them to the realm of imagination. But the intuitive system does not disappear, it simply quiets.

In Western culture especially, psychic awareness has mostly been pushed into the shadows. Over the centuries, religious doctrine labeled intuitive abilities as either delusional or demonic, while Enlightenment thinking further narrowed reality to what could be measured, tested, and repeated. This paradigm created a cultural climate in which knowing through the body, the heart, or the spirit was devalued. Rationalism became king, and any other form of perception was dismissed as fantasy or illness. But this wasn't always the case, and it still isn't in many parts of the world. In Indigenous, animist, and ancestral traditions, intuitive perception is another form of listening. The earth speaks. Ancestors whisper. The future sends ripples backward into the present. There is no hierarchy of knowing, no insistence that one form of truth must invalidate another. Instead, there is a reverence for the unseen, a trust in the body as an instrument, and a belief that perception is relational. The spirits don't speak to those who demand proof; they speak to those who pay attention.

RESEARCH INTO THE SPIRIT WORLD

As science and spirituality begin to bridge more openly, we're seeing renewed interest in the mechanics of psychic perception. Parapsychology, neuroscience, and consciousness studies are exploring how non-ordinary perception might occur. Research into remote viewing, near-death experiences, and telepathy continues to yield compelling (if controversial) data. Meanwhile, more psychologists and therapists now recognize the value of intuition and extrasensory insight in personal healing, trauma recovery, and creative breakthroughs.

The psychic experience

Despite the post-Enlightenment cultural suppression, psychic senses have found a way to persist, often through the arts, mysticism, or fringes of mainstream religion. Poets tell of visions, voices, and sudden illuminations that arrive from nowhere. Artists often speak of receiving their work rather than creating it. Mystics from every spiritual lineage describe strikingly similar phenomena: piercing insights, sudden clarity, spontaneous messages. These patterns speak to a shared human architecture, a deeper layer of perception embedded within consciousness itself.

Psychic experiences are not always dramatic or cinematic. The vast majority of intuitive impressions are subtle, quiet, and easily dismissed. A fleeting thought that proves true. A name that comes to mind before the phone rings. A feeling in the gut that something isn't quite right. These are the everyday whispers of the psychic system, the language of intuition. It rarely shouts. Instead, it nudges. It plants images, sends chills, tightens the stomach, opens the heart. To perceive it, you must learn to slow down, listen, and trust.

And therein lies the challenge: trust. Because these experiences exist outside the bounds of rational certainty, they often trigger self-doubt. Was it just a coincidence? Did I make that up? Am I being paranoid? Our cultural obsession with proof can short-circuit the subtlety of intuitive knowledge. But history tells a different story. Visions, dreams, and premonitions have shaped entire civilizations. Battles won, empires built, migrations undertaken, all on the back of a "knowing" that could not be explained, only followed.

Within spiritual communities, especially those attuned to ancestor work, divination, and ceremonial practice, psychic senses are not extraordinary, they're expected. In the Vodou, Ifá, and Espiritismo traditions, receiving messages from the spirit realm is cultivated, not questioned. It's part of the cosmology. Spirit speaks through signs, dreams, skin tingling, or a sudden gust of wind. The practitioner is trained not to doubt, but to interpret.

Still, psychic impressions are not infallible. They pass through the filter of human consciousness with all its biases, wounds, and expectations. That's why discernment is so important. Psychic perception can be incredibly accurate, but it can also be clouded by projection, fear, or wishful thinking. This is where grounding, centering, and self-inquiry come in. Without them, inner sight can become a hall of mirrors rather than a window of clarity.

Awakening the subtle senses

Spirits, whether they be ancestors, guides, deities, or other energetic beings, communicate through the subtle senses. Unlike physical conversations, these interactions often arrive as impressions, symbols, or emotional waves rather than direct speech. This is the nature of the medium: spirit communicates through the energetic field, and our psychic system is the receiver.

When a spirit is present, you may sense a shift in temperature, a particular smell, or a feeling that is difficult to explain but unmistakable. Some describe it as a sense of "presence" as if the room has become more full, more charged. Others might hear a name in their head that wasn't their own thought or feel a strong emotion that doesn't originate from their current experience. These are not figments of imagination but the vibrational language of the spirit world interpreted through the intuitive body.

In cultures where mediumship and ancestral veneration are embedded in daily life, the presence of spirit is not feared, but respected. Offerings are made. Conversations are held. Divination is used not to seek power, but to maintain the relationship. In such traditions, psychic awareness is not a gift reserved for a few, it's a faculty that is honored, cultivated, and engaged with responsibly.

How do spirits guide us?

Spirits will often reach out through dreams, one of the most accessible and universal forms of spiritual communication. In dreams, the rational mind is quieted, allowing the symbolic language of the subconscious to become primary. A departed loved one may appear with a message. A strange animal might show up repeatedly with a particular energy. You may wake with a phrase in your head or a deep emotional knowing that carries through the day. These aren't mental echoes, but energetic interactions taking place in the liminal space between worlds.

Some people experience words or phrases spoken in their inner ear. Others may feel what the spirit feels, see symbolic images or whole visions, or "know" something they have no logical way of knowing. These subtle senses are often blended, and rarely do they show up in isolation. For instance, a vision may be accompanied by a bodily sensation or an emotional shift that affirms its validity. Don't try to force a particular way of receiving, but become familiar with how information arrives uniquely for you.

Spirit interaction is not always dramatic revelations. Often, it's quiet guidance, nudges toward healing, reminders of protection, or gentle redirection when we've strayed from our path. These encounters might come when meditating, walking in nature, or even during mundane activities. That's part of the mystery: the sacred often emerges in the ordinary. The invisible world doesn't wait for ceremony, it always flows alongside us, waiting for moments of stillness or openness to make itself known.

Remember too that not all spirits are evolved, and not all messages are worth acting upon. Just as people vary in their clarity, maturity, and intention, so do entities in the spirit world. Some spirits may be confused, fragmented, or mischievous. This is why discernment and spiritual hygiene are not optional, but essential. Regular cleansing, boundary setting, and grounding practices ensure you are attuning to energies that serve your highest good. For more on developing your practice, see Part 2 of this book.

Interacting with the spirit world through your psychic senses is not about spectacle, it's about relationship. When you approach these relationships with respect, humility, and clear intention, they can become profound sources of wisdom, comfort, and personal growth. They remind us that we are never truly alone. Consciousness continues beyond the veil. Guidance is always available, not as a crutch but as a compass.

Inner sight is not something you earn, but something you uncover. It is your birthright as a being who is both matter and mystery. As you continue on your path, you'll likely find that the more you listen, the more the unseen world speaks. Not because it's been silent, but because you've remembered how to hear.

SUMMARY

- Psychic abilities (the "clairs") exist across cultures and are part of human nature.
- Subtle intuitive impressions are common entry points for spirit contact.
- You need discernment and self-awareness to interpret messages accurately.

CHAPTER 6

Psychic versus medium

Although "psychic" and "medium" are not interchangeable terms, people often conflate the two, assuming that anyone with spiritual gifts can channel spirits, or that all forms of intuitive insight come from the same source. But psychics and mediums have meaningful distinctions, which not only help clarify spiritual language, but also honor the unique energetic mechanisms of each.

What is psychic ability?

Psychic ability is fundamentally about the perception of energetic information. A psychic attunes to the subtle field surrounding all people, places, and situations – often called the auric field – and reads what is present or unfolding energetically. This may include current emotional states, unconscious beliefs, energetic imprints, or even probable timelines based on someone's current trajectory. In essence, psychics pick up on energetic patterns and interpret them in ways that bring clarity, validation, or foresight.

This kind of work is deeply relational. The psychic doesn't "see the future" in a fixed way but tunes into vibrational trends that are already in motion. A psychic reading may illuminate possibilities or potential outcomes, but it does not determine fate because of people's free will. By creating greater awareness of what is influencing the present moment, a psychic reading can help a querent make more informed or aligned decisions.

Some psychics work visually, receiving images or symbolic visions (clairvoyance). Others may receive information as direct knowing (claircognizance), or as emotional resonance (clairsentience). Some hear words or names (clairaudience), while others work through body sensations or intuition that is difficult to explain but proves accurate over time. Not all psychics are consciously aware of the specific channels they use. What matters is the integrity with which they receive and share information.

Psychics are tuning into energy that is already present in the client's field or the energetic blueprint of a situation, rather than calling in external beings or channeling outside sources. Their insight may feel uncanny or "otherworldly" in its precision, but it is still rooted in the subtle structures of the material world. A psychic might accurately describe a client's relationship patterns, identify areas of energetic stagnation, or illuminate unnamed fears, not because they are speaking with a spirit, but because they are reading the echoes and frequencies that live in the person's field.

Psychic work, then, is about accessing the energy beneath the surface of what we call reality. It brings life's invisible currents into the light so we can understand them. In this way, psychic perception becomes a tool for empowerment, not to override someone's journey, but to offer reflection, support, and resonance with what is already unfolding on their path.

While psychic abilities can support your spiritual growth and inner work, they don't automatically imply communication with spirits or the other side. That realm is the domain of mediumship, which involves a distinct focus and energetic function. Where psychics work with energy, mediums work with consciousness. The difference is subtle, but powerful.

What is mediumship?

At its core, mediumship is the art of bridging worlds – a sacred, and often humbling, experience where you open yourself to messages, impressions, and presences that exist beyond the physical realm. Contrary to pop culture portrayals, mediumship doesn't involve dramatic séances, floating objects, or whispered voices in the dark. More often, it's quiet, a flicker of insight, a sudden emotional shift, or a phrase that enters the mind out of nowhere, yet rings with unmistakable truth.

If you're called to explore mediumship, your first step isn't learning how to "hear spirits." It's learning how to listen. Deeply. Consistently. Without the constant hum of internal distraction. Spirits, particularly the dead, do not communicate in linear language or structured sentences. They communicate through symbol, sensation, emotion, and energy. Sometimes you receive a sudden memory that rushes in with no clear trigger. Other times it's a tightening in your chest, or a smell that shouldn't be there. The medium translates these subtleties with reverence and care.

One of the biggest misconceptions around mediumship is that it belongs to a select few, the "gifted" or "born with it" psychic elite. But like any intuitive ability, mediumship exists on a spectrum. Most people are capable of cultivating some form of connection if they're willing to put in the time, boundaries, and self-awareness it requires. You don't need some rare talent, just a consistent, clear, and ethical channel.

A WORD OF CAUTION

Mediumship is not for everyone. Not because it's dangerous in some superstitious sense, but because it requires a level of emotional maturity and energetic hygiene that not everyone is ready to commit to. If you are actively healing trauma, navigating grief, or experiencing instability in your personal life, attempting to channel or receive spirit communication without adequate grounding can muddy the waters, or worse, invite confusion and projection.

> Just because a spirit comes forward, you don't owe them your attention. The dead, like the living, come with a range of intentions, personalities, and levels of awareness. Some have unfinished business. Others are confused or bound. Some are simply visiting. It's not your job to fix every spirit or entertain every presence. Discernment is vital for your own well-being and for the integrity of the work.

The healthiest mediumship emerges from a place of inner clarity and emotional regulation. You need to be honest with yourself. If you're using mediumship as a way to escape your own grief or loneliness, or out of a need for validation, the messages you receive may reflect those unmet needs rather than true spiritual communication.

Before attempting any form of communication, it helps to create a ritual structure. A designated space. A clearly stated intention. A grounding practice. A method for closing the connection at the end of the session. They don't need to be elaborate or ceremonial, just consistent. Spirits recognize boundaries, and they tend to respect those who uphold them.

MEDIUMSHIP TAKES MANY FORMS

Some people experience clairaudience, hearing subtle sounds, words, or phrases internally, like a thought that doesn't quite feel like their own. Others experience clairvoyance, not literal visions, but mental imagery or symbolic flashes that arrive with a sudden sense of importance. Some feel the presence of spirit in their body, known as clairsentience – a sensation, ache, warmth, or emotional shift that doesn't originate from them.

Physical mediums channel energies that may affect their bodies directly, through involuntary movements, changes in voice, or energetic phenomena in the space around them. This form of mediumship is rarer and more intense. It requires careful training and support because it can be physically taxing and psychologically complex. Mental mediumship, where impressions, messages, or images arrive through subtle internal awareness, is more accessible for most people.

Spirit communication may also come through symbols. A recurring animal, number, song lyric, or pattern that appears in your dreams or daily life can carry meaning, particularly if it's accompanied by a strong emotional pull. Spirits often speak in symbols because the human psyche is wired to process emotion, memory, and meaning through metaphor. A feather on the ground, a flickering light, a sudden breeze are all common ways that spirits signal their presence. The medium's work is to interpret as well as observe.

The romanticism around mediumship often gets in the way of discernment. Not every "sign" is a spirit. Not every coincidence is a message. One of the great challenges of this work is learning to sit with uncertainty. A strong impression might not come with confirmation. A symbol might not make sense right away. And sometimes, you'll get nothing at all. This doesn't mean you're doing it wrong. Just like any relationship, spirit operates on its own timeline.

You must approach mediumship with humility, not as performance. You aren't a cosmic telephone operator. You are a human being with a limited, though powerful, capacity to receive. The spirits you connect with aren't props or entertainment, they are beings with often complex emotional histories and energetic imprints. Mediumship is a conversation, not a spectacle. And it requires patience.

Spirits may communicate with you in dreams before they come through in waking practice. The dreamscape is more fluid and less encumbered by rational filtering, making it a natural bridge for early messages. Pay attention to who appears, what they say, and how it feels. Emotional tone often carries more truth than literal content. A spirit who comes in love will feel different from one who arrives confused or agitated, even if they say the same words.

Dream journaling is an indispensable part of mediumship development. Over time, you'll notice recurring symbols, faces, or settings that will become the lexicon of your personal spirit communication. No dream dictionary will capture this – your symbols are yours. Building your personal map is part of becoming an accurate and ethical medium.

Who are you communicating with?

It's easy to assume that any presence is a deceased loved one, a guide, or some benevolent force. But just as in the physical world, spirits come with different intentions, personalities, and levels of awareness. Not all spirits are enlightened. Not all are wise. Some may still carry unresolved traumas, confusion, or attachment to their former lives. Others may not be human in origin. This isn't a cause for fear, but for clarity. You have the right to question, pause, and even decline communication. Just because a spirit can come through doesn't mean it should.

A foundational part of safe mediumship is being able to say "no." To close the session. To set a firm boundary. This is especially true for empaths and highly sensitive people, who may feel obliged to stay open out of compassion or curiosity. But mediumship is not a constant state. You aren't meant to walk through the world as a permanently open channel. Learn to close the door.

At first you may doubt the messages. You may feel like you're making it up. That's normal. Trust in yourself. It takes time to differentiate between imagination and intuition. The key is noticing how the message lands. Does it carry a charge? Does it stir emotion or bring clarity? Spirit communication often comes with a physical resonance, a chill down the spine, tears welling unexpectedly, a sudden sense of stillness. These subtle but telling signs indicate something true is passing through.

During my own early development, I was sitting in quiet meditation, not expecting anything significant, when I suddenly felt the room shift. The air thickened and I got the sense I wasn't alone. A presence formed behind me, firm but not menacing. I didn't hear words exactly, but a thought pressed into my mind: *Tell her I'm proud of her.* It made no sense in the moment. I wasn't even doing a reading. But I wrote it down.

The next day, a friend mentioned that her grandmother had passed. On impulse, I asked, "Did she ever say she was proud of you?" My friend froze, eyes wide. She told me those were the words she had longed to hear in life but never received. I shared the message. We both had chills and became flooded with emotion. It was a turning point, not because it was flashy, but because it mattered. That's the heart of mediumship. However, it was only because she was a friend that I shared the message on impulse. Had the message been for a stranger, I may have considered it would not be acceptable to share something so personal without consent.

Mediumship not about proving anything. It's not about theatrical performances or "wow" moments. It's about healing. Connection. Closure. Validation. When practiced with integrity, spirit communication can be one of the most deeply human and humbling experiences you can offer or receive. But it must come from a grounded place, one rooted in ethics, preparation, and reverence.

Keep a spiritual hygiene practice. Make offerings if that aligns with your tradition. Journal everything. Study, but also feel. You're building a relationship with the spirits as well as your own ability to trust what moves through you. And like all relationships, it takes time, consistency, and respect.

Above all else, remember that mediumship is about presence. You're not meant to be a flawless conduit. You're meant to show up, open-hearted, curious, and grounded in your truth. That is enough. And in time, it becomes more than enough.

SUMMARY

- Psychics read energy fields and patterns from people and places.
- Mediums communicate with spirits or non-physical consciousness.
- All mediums are psychic, but not all psychics are mediums; know your strengths.

PART 2

DEVELOPING A PRACTICE FOR WORKING WITH SPIRITS

CHAPTER 7

Foundations of a good practice

A strong spiritual connection does not appear overnight. Like any other skill or relationship, it requires cultivation. The foundation of a solid practice begins with yourself: your discipline, mindset, and clarity of intention. At the heart of a good practice is consistency. The spirit world responds to regular, meaningful presence more than dramatic gestures. Whether your practice includes daily meditation, weekly offerings, or seasonal rituals, consistency builds trust and momentum. Spirits engage more deeply with those who show up over time, not just when it's convenient or in a crisis. In the pages that follow, I've detailed nine foundations of a good practice. You may find more yourself as you develop your own practice.

SILENCE IS GOLDEN

Create space in your life for silence. We are constantly surrounded by noise: mental, emotional, and digital. Spirit communication is subtle. If you want to hear more clearly, you need to quiet the interference. You don't need to meditate for an hour a day, just give yourself the grace to unplug and notice. Your energy is a doorway. How you care for that doorway affects what comes through.

1. Ethics and integrity

A good spiritual practice is built on a foundation of ethics and integrity. This means taking full responsibility for how you engage with the unseen. Working with spirits is a relationship, and relationships require reciprocity. Ask yourself: Am I approaching this work with respect? Am I listening as much as I'm asking? Am I taking without giving anything back?

It's not uncommon for people to want quick results – guidance, healing, protection – but spirits aren't vending machines. A one-sided dynamic can quickly lead to imbalance. Offerings, gratitude, and follow-through matter. Even if a spirit is nonverbal or ancestral, they often respond to acts of respect: a bowl of water, a candle lit in their name, words spoken from the heart, or a promise fulfilled. Having a good practice means remembering this work is mutual.

2. Intention

Intention shapes the tone of your work. Without clear intention, even the most beautifully structured ritual can fall flat. What are you hoping to learn, offer, or transform? Ask this question frequently as your practice evolves. Vague curiosity can open doors you're not ready to walk through. A grounded, humble, and curious mindset is far more effective than a craving for power or spectacle.

3. Spiritual hygiene

Just as you clean your physical body and home, your energetic space requires upkeep. This includes regularly cleansing your altar, aura, and home, whether through smoke, sound, salt, or visualization. It's not superstition to clear residual energy, especially after intense emotional exchanges or spiritual work, it's maintenance.

Spiritual hygiene also includes regulating your nervous system. Many people seek spiritual connection to escape from anxiety or overwhelm.

But working with spirits from a dysregulated, overly anxious, fearful, or emotionally reactive state can distort your perception and leave you vulnerable. A good practice includes grounding techniques, breathwork, and rest. You do not need to be "perfectly calm" to engage, but the more centered and embodied you are, the more clearly you'll perceive.

Emotional hygiene is just as critical as spiritual hygiene. Spirit work amplifies what's already present within you. If you're feeling ungrounded, anxious, or reactive, those states can color how you interpret messages and what you attract. You don't need to be emotionally perfect, no one is, but be self-aware enough to pause when needed. Some of the most profound spiritual clarity comes after moments of emotional stillness.

4. Discernment

This is non-negotiable. Not every spirit who appears is helpful, and not every message is worth following. You are allowed – in fact required – to question, test, and protect your space. A good practice is protected as well as open. Discernment includes setting firm energetic boundaries, developing internal signals for "yes" and "no," and being willing to say, "Not right now." Spirits don't have ultimate authority, you do.

As you deepen into spiritual work, discernment is one of the most essential, and often overlooked, foundations. This skill grows through experience, self-awareness, and patience. It includes the ability to say, "I don't know yet," and the humility to seek confirmation before acting. You might check in with a divination tool, ask a trusted practitioner for a second perspective, or wait for a message to repeat itself in a different form. Spirit work doesn't always reward speed, but it rewards clarity, consistency, and presence.

5. Self-inquiry

Just as important as divination or rituals is self-inquiry. The deeper your inner awareness, the more stable your practice becomes. Ask yourself regularly: Why am I doing this work? What am I avoiding? What am I trying to prove? These questions are meant to keep you honest. Many people unconsciously use spirit work to bypass emotional pain or escape responsibility. A good practice requires that you stay present with your humanity while you explore your spirituality.

Respect your capacity. A good practice does not demand constant engagement or spiritual labor. Some periods will be more active, others more reflective. Honor your ebbs and flows without guilt. Forcing connection when you're burned out or emotionally overwhelmed usually leads to confusion or misinterpretation. A sustainable practice includes rest, play, and mundane living.

It's a myth that you need to be "on" all the time to be spiritual. You don't. Spirit work has seasons. Sometimes the work is active, full of messages and synchronicities. Other times it goes quiet. That doesn't mean something's wrong. It means you're integrating. Let those quieter times nourish you. You are a human being, not a spiritual vending machine.

6. Structure and consistency

Structure means having a clear rhythm and containment for your work. This might look like setting aside a specific day each week for practicing deeper ritual or keeping a dedicated altar space where interactions take place. Maybe you use the same opening invocation every time you sit in meditation, or close each session with a grounding practice. Structure helps your nervous system feel safe, and it signals to spirits that you're approaching them with intention.

Ritual is a way of creating energetic consistency. Lighting a candle at the same time each evening, offering a glass of water to your guides every Sunday, or opening your sacred space with the same invocation each time all create resonance and continuity. Spirits recognize patterns. They come to understand your rhythms and your sincerity. The more consistent you are, the clearer the channel becomes.

7. Consensual engagement

Just as you wouldn't want someone barging into your home uninvited, spirits – especially ancestors, land spirits, or nonhuman intelligences – respond better when you approach them with courtesy. Before invoking or calling anything in, ask: Is this relationship wanted on both sides? Am I prepared to tend it responsibly? Just because you can make contact doesn't mean you should. Respectful and consensual engagement creates clean energetic lines and prevents unnecessary entanglements.

8. Reverence

A good practice includes reverence. That doesn't mean worship. It means respect. When you work with spirits, you're engaging with sentient consciousness. You are not entitled to their time, energy, or presence. You are building relationships. And that means approaching your work with care, consistency, and humility. You don't need to know everything to begin. You just need to begin in a way that's honest, grounded, and aligned with who you are right now.

9. Community

Finally, community can offer both protection and perspective. While solitary practice is valid and powerful, isolation can breed confusion or ego traps. A good practice does not need to be secretive or performative. Having one or two trusted peers, people you can process experiences with or who will call you back to center, is an invaluable support.

Creating rituals

Your spirit work practice doesn't begin with a fancy altar, a long lineage, or a list of spirits you hope to call on. It begins with the relationship you have with yourself, your intuition, energy field, and integrity. Every practitioner must build a spiritual container strong enough to hold their experiences. This container isn't physical. It's energetic. It's made of your clarity, boundaries, emotional resilience, and ability to stay present. These are your true tools.

Rituals don't have to be elaborate. A simple practice done regularly will strengthen your connection with the spirit world more than something you only do when you're in the mood or when things go wrong.

Start by making space for spirit work. That might mean a few minutes of grounding each morning, or journaling your dreams, or doing a light cleanse of your room before you go to sleep. You are telling the spirit world, "I'm available. I'm paying attention. I'm creating a channel." This consistency strengthens your signal.

As you build a solid foundation, check in with yourself often. Are you grounded? Are you hydrated? Have you eaten? Are you working from a clear state, or are you stressed and trying to force something to happen? Spirit work will mirror your internal state. If you are scattered, the messages will feel scattered, but if you are rooted, you'll find that the messages are clearer. Building your foundation will help you become a more reliable receiver.

Remember, what works for you in your first year may not serve you five years down the line. That's growth. Let your practice breathe. Let it shift. Let yourself outgrow tools or techniques that no longer align. Your spiritual path is alive, and so are the spirits you work with. A strong foundation doesn't mean things stay the same, it means you have the strength and clarity to meet change with trust.

Finding what resonates

It can be easy to be pulled into ideas of the "right way" to practice or which spirits to connect with, especially when online trends or voices dominate the conversation. But alignment and authenticity matter far more in spirit work than appearance or imitation.

A practice rooted in tradition should also be rooted in personal connection. If you feel drawn to deities, spirits, or belief systems from cultural traditions that are unfamiliar to you, take time to reflect on what draws you in. Is it something that resonates deeply with your spirit and values, or is it coming from curiosity, aesthetic appeal, or external influence?

There is no one-size-fits-all path. Even in open traditions, ask yourself why you are drawn to something and whether it reflects your own ancestry, values, or spiritual guidance. Sometimes the most meaningful work comes from exploring your own heritage, lineage, or the land you live on now. It means you are building something sustainable.

In my experience, spirits respond to truth. Not performance, not externally validated spirituality, not dogma. Just genuine, grounded intention.

In other words, don't seek to work with certain spirits or adopt a practice because of how you'll be perceived. I started working with local land spirits and my spirit guides, who were cosmic beings, long before I even considered working with deities. You will find far more connection and clarity when your practice feels like your own, rather than someone else's projection. This work is personal. It does not need to be validated by strangers. And if something does not resonate, you do not need permission to let it go.

SUMMARY

- You need a consistent and grounded spiritual practice for safety and growth.
- The goal is not power or escape, but self-awareness, clarity, and responsibility.
- Blind belief in spirits or systems can be dangerous without critical thinking.
- Developing trust in your own experience is part of building a strong foundation.

CHAPTER 8

Grounding, shielding, and centering

Psychic and energetic sensitivity can be as destabilizing as it is illuminating. Throughout cultures and traditions, spiritual practitioners have evolved techniques for managing, containing, and directing energy not just for magical efficacy, but for survival. Before you open, you must first be anchored. Before inviting connection, you must establish boundaries. These practices aren't new; grounding, shielding, and centering have always been the quiet, necessary foundations beneath even the most extraordinary workings.

In ancient Greece, initiates into the Eleusinian Mysteries underwent ritual purifications that included fasting, bathing, and grounding connection to the earth through sacred processionals. Many Indigenous cultures emphasize the relationship with land, roots, and body as central to the daily practice of spiritual life. The body is not a vessel to escape, but a sacred tool; maintaining presence in the body is a core value for safe spiritual work.

Grounding

Of the three practices, grounding is perhaps the most vital. At its heart, grounding is the process of anchoring your energetic awareness into something stable, often the earth but not always. This concept finds resonance in many traditions: in Taoism, qi (life force) is harmonized through posture and breath connected to the earth; in yoga, the root chakra (muladhara) is the seat of stability, physicality, and survival instincts. Grounding thus draws your attention and energy out of the mental and emotional noise of the upper chakras and reconnects you with presence, stillness, and embodiment.

In modern practice, grounding extends beyond visualizing roots in the earth to include embodied movement practices, mindful eating, maintaining a relationship with nature, and engaging in mundane or "earthy" tasks.

GROUNDING RITUALS

Grounding is about energetic downward flow. It can drain excess stimulation, restore calm, and allow for a clean reset of the nervous system. Activities like tending a garden, cleaning your living space, or walking with attention on your breath and footfalls are all grounding rituals. For highly empathic or psychically sensitive individuals, you may need to practice grounding several times a day, especially after intense energetic exchange or spiritual work.

Modern trauma-informed approaches to spirituality recognize that ungrounded spiritual practice can replicate patterns of disassociation. Escaping the body to seek higher planes may feel relieving if you're carrying unresolved trauma, but ultimately, you risk reinforcing a split among mind, body, and spirit. Grounding helps close that gap. It teaches us that the divine is not "out there" but present in every breath, bone, and grounded heartbeat.

More than just a spiritual hygiene practice, grounding anchors your awareness in the body and keeps your energy steady, no matter what's happening around you. When you connect with spirit, the experience can be expansive, emotional, even disorienting. Grounding helps you return to a state of clarity and presence after those interactions. It acts as a stabilizer, so you're not overwhelmed by energy that isn't yours or lost in the intangible.

In spirit work, your body is the vessel. It's where information gets translated, whether through sensation, intuition, or subtle impressions. If you're ungrounded, it's like trying to pour water into a cup that's tipping over. Grounding ensures your vessel is upright, strong, and ready to hold what's coming through. It also helps you discern between real energetic information and your own emotional noise. Without grounding, it's easy to mistake anxiety for intuitive messages or get swept up in someone else's emotional current. Anchoring yourself lets you filter what's truly meaningful from what's just passing through. Some spirits, especially those connected to the land, respond more readily to people who are grounded. Being grounded shows you respect the balance between the energetic and the physical, and you're not bypassing your role as a human channel for the work.

Shielding

In contrast, shielding is a protective measure. The concept of "banishing" or warding against unwanted energy has been part of magical traditions for centuries. Protective circles, amulets, and wards are all examples of externalized shielding, but the most powerful shield often begins internally. When you build energetic resilience, learn to recognize what is yours and what is not, and establish intentional space, you begin to shape your energetic field consciously, rather than reactively.

Shielding isn't a static structure. A rigid, overused shield can numb your sensitivity or create spiritual isolation. Ideally, shielding should be dynamic, expanding, or contracting depending on context. On a crowded train, your shield might be firm, reflective, and close. In a sacred space among trusted allies, it might soften and become more porous.

With time, you'll learn to adjust the tone, density, and responsiveness of your shield like tuning an instrument.

Energetically speaking, shielding often draws from the solar plexus, your center of power and agency. From here, you can assert boundaries through visualization, intention, tone of voice, posture, and presence. The most effective shield begins from within: a deep, confident knowing of your own worth and a refusal to let external energies dictate your state.

Therefore, shielding is the art of energetic protection, not from a place of fear but from self-respect. The practice reinforces your autonomy as a spiritual practitioner and helps you remain sovereign in all interactions, including those with spirits. Shielding doesn't mean walling yourself off or rejecting connection. It means filtering out what doesn't serve you and holding space for what does.

When you shield, you are stating energetically: "This is my space. This is my field. I decide what enters." That level of clarity sends a strong signal across spiritual planes and deters uninvited energies from latching on. It also keeps your intuitive field cleaner, so what you do receive is more accurate and less distorted.

HOW AND WHEN TO SHIELD YOURSELF

There are many ways to shield, but the most effective one is the one you actually practice. Here are some shields for you to experiment with:

- **Visualization** Imagine a sphere of white or golden light surrounding your body, expanding from your core and sealing your energy. You might visualize a cloak or a mirrored surface protecting you.
- **Spoken charm** Say aloud or internally, "I am protected by light and truth. All that is not mine is returned to its source. Only what serves my highest good may enter." You can repeat this during your morning routine, before entering a charged environment, or prior to spiritual work.
- **Protective symbol** Wear or inscribe symbols like the pentacle, hamsa, or Algiz rune on your body or jewelry. These are historically rooted symbols of spiritual defense, used in traditions from Norse to Middle Eastern and Western ceremonial practices. I encourage you to work with symbols that resonate with your personal practice, ancestry, or spiritual path.

» **Gesture** Trace a pentacle in the air before you with your hand or finger, or press your thumb to your sternum three times while focusing on sealing or shielding your energy. What matters is repeating the gesture consistently with purpose, focus, and intent.

Your shield can be as simple or as elaborate as your path requires. The key is the sincerity behind the act.

Shielding is especially important before spiritual rituals, visiting crowded or emotionally intense environments, or after having deep conversations. Even social media can carry energetic residue. When your field has picked up something that isn't yours, you'll begin to notice subtle shifts such as fatigue, irritability, or mood swings. That's your cue to reinforce your shield.

Remember, shielding isn't permanent. Like brushing your teeth or grounding your energy, it's a regular maintenance task. With consistency, shielding becomes second nature. You won't always need to pause and visualize, your energy field will eventually adapt to hold that frequency naturally.

Spirits, especially unfamiliar ones, often test boundaries to gauge your readiness or intention. Having clear shielding in place ensures you're stepping into communication from a place of empowerment, not vulnerability. It says, "I respect this work and myself enough to protect what matters."

Centering

The final component is centering. More than being calm or balanced, being centered is returning to the core of your being. It is a spiritual homecoming. When you center, you draw your awareness inward and downward, into the place within you that is still, sovereign, and unchanged by external fluctuations. Some traditions refer to this place as the "inner sanctuary" or "seat of the soul." When centered, your actions flow from this place of clarity rather than chaos.

If grounding connects us to the earth and shielding defines our boundaries, centering brings us into a conscious relationship with ourselves. It's the practice of returning, again and again, to the quiet, steady place at the heart of your being. During energetic work, centering helps you access your inner compass. It's the voice that says, "This is me," even when the energetic landscape around you is chaotic, emotional, or charged.

WAYS TO CENTER YOURSELF

1. **Breath** Practice a slow inhale and exhale that drops awareness into the belly.

2. **Visualization** Focus on a sensation you feel in the chest or visualize a flame in your heart center.

3. **Drawing in energy** Draw energy into your *hara* or *dantian* (energetic centers in Japanese and Chinese traditions, respectively) to cultivate an inner gravity that steadies the whole field.

Regardless of the method, the goal is the same: return to the seat of the self and operate from there.

During energetic work, you may be in communication with multiple energetic influences, subtle impressions, or even intense spiritual sensations. Without a strong sense of center, it becomes difficult to determine what is yours and what is coming from elsewhere. Centering allows you to engage with spirits without being consumed by them. It helps you witness the experience, rather than be overwhelmed by it.

Some practitioners describe centering like an unwavering flame at the heart of the body. You can return to that flame any time you feel scattered, anxious, overextended, or entangled in someone else's field. When you are centered, you can speak with your own voice, rather than echoing what's been projected onto you.

Centering supports the integration of your practice. It brings all parts of you – mind, body, spirit – into a cohesive whole. This cohesion strengthens your boundaries, increases your psychic sensitivity, and deepens your intuitive knowing. Think of it like spiritual gravity. When you are centered, everything else orients itself more clearly around you.

SUMMARY

In modern esoteric circles, grounding, shielding, and centering are often taught early, sometimes so early that they're rushed or minimized. But they are not beginner techniques, they are master practices. The more sensitive, open, or skilled you become, the more essential these tools are. You can channel brilliantly or see clearly, but without grounding, shielding, and centering, your body will eventually show signs of overload, confusion, or depletion.

- Grounding anchors your energy and helps you stay present and stable.
- Shielding protects your energetic boundaries from interference or unwanted contact.
- Centering helps you align your focus and energy before spirit work.
- These techniques are fundamental to spiritual protection and clarity.

CHAPTER 9

Protection, discernment, and ethical spirit contact

Working with spirit isn't just about opening to unseen realms, it's also about learning how to move through them with clarity and sovereignty. Not every message is sacred. Not every energy has your best interest at heart. And not every invitation should be accepted. This chapter explores the tools and mindsets you need to navigate spiritual contact with integrity, safety, and a grounded sense of ethics. Here are eight steps to safe, ethical spiritual encounters.

1. Protect yourself

The idea of psychic protection can sound dramatic, conjuring images of demons or attacks, but in truth, it's much simpler. Protection is about energetic hygiene. It's about boundaries. You wouldn't walk into a crowded train station and let every stranger speak into your ear, touch your body, or give you unsolicited advice. And yet, that's what some people do energetically when they begin working with spirit without preparation. Protection helps filter what comes through.

It starts with your intention. Before you engage in any kind of spirit contact, whether it's a meditation, a reading, or simply tuning in, set a clear boundary. Speak it aloud if that helps: "I am open to connecting only with energies and spirits that are aligned with truth, healing, and my highest good." More than a formality, this shapes the energetic container you're working within. Spirits respond to clarity, and setting an intention helps ward off those who don't align with it.

Energetic protection comes in many forms. Some people visualize themselves surrounded by a sphere of white or golden light. Others invoke specific guides, deities, or ancestral allies to hold space and safeguard the encounter. You might wear protective talismans or work with herbs and stones known for their shielding properties: black tourmaline, obsidian, mugwort, rue. The method you use is less important than the conviction behind it. What matters is being intentional and consistent.

2. Practice discernment

Just as crucial as protection is discernment. It's one thing to allow spirit contact; it's another to understand what you're receiving. Your critical thinking must walk hand-in-hand with intuition. When you receive a vivid image, phrase, or deep sense of knowing, ask yourself: Where is this coming from? Does it align with what I know to be true? Is it loving? Is it manipulative? Not every spirit who speaks with conviction is wise. Not every entity who says they're "a guide" is here to help. Learn to examine the energy behind the message as well as the message itself.

One of the biggest red flags in spirit communication is urgency or fear. Any message that pressures you to *"do this now or something bad will happen"* deserves pause. Benevolent spirits respect free will. They may offer nudges, wisdom, or warnings, but they do not coerce. They do not demand. When in doubt, step back. You're allowed to close the session, take time, and ask for further clarification. Spirit work is a dialogue, not a one-way street.

FALSE FLAGS

In my practice, I've encountered energies that were clever, polished, even flattering, but subtly disruptive. One in particular came through during a period of grief, presenting itself as a lost loved one. The tone was just slightly off, but the message pulled at my guilt and sorrow, urging me toward rash decisions. When I sat with it, meditated, and asked my guides to step in, the presence lifted. What remained was the unmistakable sense that something had been masquerading, feeding on my emotional vulnerability. This experience taught me that even in sacred work, you must sharpen discernment like a blade.

3. Cultivate your inner landscape

A key element of safe and ethical spirit contact is understanding your own inner landscape. Many people mistake their internal psychological projections for external spiritual messages. That doesn't make the experience invalid, but it does mean we must develop self-awareness as a tool of spiritual clarity. Are you hearing a message, or is it your anxiety speaking? Are you feeling a presence, or are you sensing unresolved trauma in your body? Spirit work doesn't bypass our inner world, but brings us face-to-face with it. The clearer we are about what's ours, the clearer we can be about what's not.

Regular practices like journaling, grounding, and energy-clearing help you stay anchored. When you know how your body and energy feel on an average day, it becomes easier to detect when something unusual is present. Spirit contact often feels distinct: subtle but charged with a quality that is "other." It may enter gently, like a shift in pressure in the room, a tingling in your crown, or an emotion that isn't yours. With time, you'll learn the difference between your intuition and your instinct, between a guide's gentle nudge and your own wishful thinking.

4. Set boundaries

Boundaries are just as essential in the spirit world as they are in our daily lives. You have the right to say "no." You have the right to end communication at any time. If persistent spirits are waking you up night after night, that's not a badge of honor, it's a boundary issue. You're not obliged to be open 24/7 just because you're sensitive. Imagine if your house had no door – anyone could walk in at any time, whether you were ready or not. Being spiritually open doesn't mean being spiritually exposed. Create "office hours" if necessary. Speak aloud: "I am only available for contact during intentional, respectful practice. You are not welcome to disturb my rest."

5. Act ethically

The moment you engage in spirit work, especially on behalf of others, you're entering sacred territory. Integrity isn't optional, it's the foundation. Just because you can access information doesn't mean you should share it. Just because you feel something doesn't mean you're obliged to act on it. Part of ethical spirit contact means obtaining consent, from both the person you're working with and the spirit you're engaging. Do not invoke, summon, or interact with spirits without their permission, especially if they are ancestral or culturally specific entities that are not part of your lineage or training.

The same goes for mediumship and psychic readings. If someone hasn't asked for a message, don't deliver one. Spirit might show you something about a stranger on the street, but that doesn't mean it's your place to intervene. Sometimes spirit teaches us by revealing something we must choose not to act on. Part of your role as a developing intuitive is learning what to do with the information you receive.

When you speak on behalf of a spirit, especially publicly or professionally, it's your responsibility to be as clear and respectful as possible. Avoid dramatization. Avoid assuming full understanding. Say what you received but be honest about what you don't know. Don't embellish. Don't inflate. And don't treat spirit contact like a parlor trick. It isn't. It's a relationship, and one that requires care.

6. Keep relationships healthy

Healthy spiritual dynamics are mutual, balanced, and based on respect. A true spirit guide will never coerce, frighten, or manipulate you. They may challenge you but shouldn't override your agency or instill fear. If a spirit demands constant attention, isolates you from others, or pressures you into secrecy, these are red flags. Trust your gut. The spirit world is vast. There are tricksters, fragments, and opportunistic entities along with loving, evolved guides. That's why discernment is your compass.

Don't be afraid to seek help when needed. If a spiritual encounter leaves you feeling unwell, emotionally distressed, or energetically drained, reach out to a trusted mentor, a spiritual practitioner, or even a therapist with experience in spiritual emergence. You're not expected to navigate every encounter alone. In fact, spiritual isolation can create real harm. You deserve support.

7. Maintain your sovereignty

Sovereignty is a word often used in magical and spiritual circles, but what does it actually mean? At its core, sovereignty means you are the authority in your life. Even as you open to guidance from spirit, ancestors, or intuition, you should never surrender your autonomy. Sovereignty isn't the absence of influence but the conscious navigation of it. It's the difference between being led and being manipulated.

This is especially important when people begin receiving channeled messages. Spirit can offer insight, but you are still the final interpreter. You are responsible to vet what you receive, to hold it up to the light of your own knowing, your ethics, and your lived reality. Practice and personal development matter. The clearer your inner compass, the more trustworthy your spiritual navigation becomes.

It can be tempting, especially in early spirit contact, to rely overly on external messages, to ask spirit for guidance on everything from what to eat to who to trust. But that's not the goal. Spirit guides don't want to run your life. They want to help you become more aligned with your own wisdom. True guidance is a mirror, not a leash.

8. Stay humble

Finally, a reminder that humility is part of protection. If you approach the spirit world with entitlement, bravado, or the illusion that you already know everything, you may get in over your head. But if you approach with reverence, curiosity, and care, you're more likely to build lasting, reciprocal relationships that nourish you over time. Spirit work is not about domination, it's about listening. It's about connection. It's about growth.

You don't need to be perfect to walk this path. But you do need to be honest. Stay grounded. Stay curious. And most of all, stay connected: to your body, your values, and the living world around you. That's where your greatest protection lives.

Understanding spiritual interference

Spiritual interference is often sensationalized, skewed by movies, pop culture, or fear-based teachings that portray the spirit world as a constant battleground between light and darkness. In reality, spiritual interference is far more nuanced and often much less dramatic. That doesn't mean it should be dismissed, but that understanding it requires clarity, not paranoia.

At its core, spiritual interference refers to any outside energetic or spiritual influence that disrupts a person's clarity, sovereignty, or well-being. These influences may stem from many sources: residual energy, unhealed emotional cords, ancestral imprints, thought-forms, or lower-vibrational entities. They can be temporary or chronic, subtle or intense. But not all spiritual discomfort stems from interference, and not all interference is malicious. Often, it's simply unresolved energy looking for a place to land.

People may feel "off," foggy, reactive, or disoriented without any clear physical cause. In these instances, your automatic assumption may be to blame a spirit or "entity." But sometimes, it's unprocessed trauma, burnout, or even your diet. The human nervous system is highly sensitive, and as spirit workers or intuitives, we learn quickly that not everything is spiritual. But we should also learn how to recognize when something is.

Energetic boundaries are your first line of defense. Without them, you become porous, absorbing impressions and imbalances from others like a sponge. Spiritual beings are not always invading someone's space. Sometimes it's the weight of someone else's grief, anxiety, or anger attaching to our field like static cling. When left unchecked, this build-up can attract opportunistic spiritual interference, not necessarily because you're "under attack," but because something in your field is resonating with that same frequency.

Spiritual interference doesn't always announce itself. It often comes in quietly, piggybacking on moments of vulnerability, grief, trauma, substance use, or spiritual overextension. In some cases, people who've recently experienced significant upheaval – such as a loss, a breakup, a move, or even a spiritual awakening – may notice a shift in their energy. They might feel like they've "picked something up," or that their intuition has gone fuzzy.

Signs of interference

Common signs of spiritual interference include:

- recurring intrusive thoughts that don't feel like yours
- sudden and uncharacteristic mood swings
- recurring energetic exhaustion despite rest
- feeling watched or accompanied when alone
- dreams that become distorted or fragmented
- synchronicities suddenly turning sour
- messages that are harder to interpret
- symbols that once felt affirming now feeling confusing or void.

A common pattern is a sort of psychic static, an almost imperceptible fog that sets in, clouding clarity and making people second-guess their intuitive hits.

This subtle disorientation can lead people to reach for more and more tools, readings, or rituals in an effort to "clear it," sometimes digging themselves deeper into energetic dependency loops.

Remember, not all spiritual interference is active or sentient. Most interference is more akin to energetic residue: leftovers from emotionally charged situations, environments, or people. These residues can hang in a space, cling to a person's auric field, or even echo through ancestral lines. Energetically sensitive people might pick up on these impressions without realizing they don't belong to them.

KIRA'S STORY

For months Kira, a woman I once worked with, had been feeling haunted by a low-level unease. She described a persistent inner monologue that questioned her worth, disrupted her sleep, and made her doubt her spiritual path. At first she thought it was old trauma resurfacing, and she approached it through therapy and inner-child work. But the voice lingered. She said it felt foreign, like something inserted into her energy rather than arising from within.

When we sat down together, it became clear that this wasn't just psychological, it was energetic. She had recently visited an old family home, which had stirred up ancestral imprints, including grief and rage that had never been spoken aloud. Kira had unknowingly become a carrier for these unresolved energies, and because she was emotionally open and highly empathic, her body and psyche became a container for them.

Clearing the interference didn't involve banishing or a battle, but acknowledgment. Through ritual, journaling, and ancestral veneration, Kira began to witness the pain, honor it, and release what didn't belong to her. Within days, her unease softened, and within weeks, it was gone. Her dreams shifted from chaos to clarity and her intuition returned, stronger than before.

This story isn't unusual. Many people experience spiritual interference not because they are "attacked" but because they are unconsciously resonating with energies that need acknowledgment or release. While some interferences are more stubborn, most respond to presence, clarity, and boundaries.

Discernment is the linchpin of all spiritual work. Spiritual interference, like anything energetic, is easy to mislabel when we're operating from a place of fear, projection, or ego.

It's important to be able to pause and ask: Is this mine? It sounds simple, but this question can cut through layers of confusion. Many energetically sensitive people are trained, even unconsciously, to merge. They feel everything – other people's pain, environmental pressure, and collective energies – which they internalize as personal. Asking whether something belongs to you energetically gives you an opportunity to reclaim your own space and let go of what doesn't serve you.

You're not doing something wrong

A pervasive myth is that spiritual interference only happens to those who are "doing something wrong," as if someone's energy field is breached because they're undisciplined or careless. The truth is, being human means being porous. We are constantly interfacing with each other, with space, with memory, with spirit. Sometimes, what we're experiencing isn't interference in the way we think, but a call to refine our clarity, or engage in a deeper layer of personal work.

An unhelpful tendency in some circles is to default to "attack" language, describing every interference as a hex, psychic attack, or malevolent entity. While those experiences do happen, they are relatively rare; framing every energetic disruption as a battle can cultivate paranoia and disempowerment. A more grounded approach is to treat the moment as information: a nudge that something in your field, habits, or environment needs attention.

That said, sovereignty is non-negotiable. If you feel something in your field that doesn't belong, whether it's an ancestral echo, an energetic hitchhiker, or a thought-form that's latched on, you can revoke permission and remove it. This doesn't require an elaborate ritual or specific tradition. Reclaim your space by stating clearly and with conviction: "You are not welcome here. I do not consent to your presence. You must leave now."

Sometimes it helps to accompany this with a physical clearing: smoke, sound, salt, prayer, water, or movement. But mostly the clarity of your will does the work. You are the threshold. Your body, energy, and mind are all sacred spaces and you have the right to tend them.

Ultimately, spiritual interference isn't a sign you're failing. It indicates you're deepening your awareness, learning to navigate with more subtlety, confidence, and energetic hygiene. As with any spiritual challenge, the lesson is not to fear but to refine. To notice the friction, investigate the cause, and return to center.

The more we practice energetic sovereignty, the less vulnerable we become because we've cultivated the tools and clarity to respond instead of react. More than anything, that is what turns a sensitive person into a powerful practitioner.

SUMMARY

- Protection involves both energetic and practical boundaries.
- Discernment means questioning what you experience, not just believing it blindly.
- Ethics in spirit work include consent, respect, and not overstepping your role.
- Not every spirit or message should be trusted without evaluation.

CHAPTER 10

Petition and reciprocity

From ancient ancestor veneration to saintly intercession, spirit communication has taken countless forms across cultures, belief systems, and eras. Building a relationship with spirit is about acknowledging that consciousness exists beyond the veil of the physical, which can respond, observe, or even participate in our world.

In my own journey, which blends threads of mysticism, ancestral reverence, ceremonial magic, and modern psychic development, I've come to understand spirit as a spectrum of presence. Along with spirits of the dead, we are surrounded by spirits of place, spirits of nature, archetypal energies, guides, guardians, and intelligences that don't fit neatly into any singular tradition. Relationship-building is a way of honoring this multiplicity without requiring it to conform to our expectations.

In traditional African spiritual systems, such as Yoruba and its diasporic offshoots Santería and Candomblé, devotees forge relationships over time with spirits, known as orishas, through offerings, songs, and formal initiations. These spirits aren't abstract forces but living intelligences, each with specific personalities, preferences, and areas of influence. Petitioning is a matter of protocol and respect. You don't simply demand, but approach with reverence, often under the guidance of a trained elder. Within these practices, spirit communication is not extraordinary, but something woven into the fabric of everyday life.

In folk Catholicism and other Christian mystic practices, spirits may take the form of saints or angels. Followers offer petitions through novenas, candles, prayers, and altars. These figures often represent specific aspects of life, such as Saint Anthony for lost things, Saint Jude for hopeless causes, and Saint Michael for protection. Though formal Christian doctrine may resist the idea of "spirit work," everyday practitioners understand that the saints move between worlds, responding to faithful invocation.

Similarly in East Asian traditions, people honor the spirits of family members at ancestor altars through incense, food, and bowing. In these spaces, relationships are everything. Frequency of presence matters. The spirit is part of the home, part of the rhythm of life.

What these traditions share is the understanding that spirit responds to relationship, not to force.

Connection is not instant but is built through consistency, acknowledgment, and intention. While the ways we open the conversation may differ – through candlelight, chanting, prayer, sigil, or silent thought – the fundamental act is the same: we reach out in recognition of another intelligence.

In my own practice, I've come to see that spirits speak many languages. Visual symbols. A scent, sound, or wave of presence that moves through the room like a hush. Or silence, which can be as meaningful as a sign. What remains constant is the shift in energy that comes with real connection. You don't need to "believe" in a spirit for it to make itself known. You only need to approach with openness and a willingness to listen.

There's a distinction between sensing the presence of spirit and forming a relationship with it. The latter requires time, intention, and discernment. It's a dance of mutual recognition, learning how your energy interacts with theirs, and discovering what language feels most resonant between you.

In various traditions, the act of petitioning is a sacred exchange, which is relational rather than transactional. Whether it's placing a glass of water before an ancestor photo or lighting incense with whispered words, what matters most is the sincerity of the approach. Spirit responds to clarity, frequency, and humility. More than asking for things, petitioning is about stepping into a deeper current of communication, where messages flow both ways and the boundaries between the seen and unseen soften in subtle but powerful ways.

Petition, presence, and the spirit of reciprocity

While "petition" may sound formal or archaic, the word describes intentional communication, the act of addressing a spirit with a specific request, offering, or message. While this act has taken many forms across traditions, what's striking is that all emphasize clarity, humility, and reciprocity. You do not coerce spirit. You invite, acknowledge, or request. And in turn, you pay attention.

In ancient Roman religion, household spirits were known as the Lares and Penates. These domestic spirits were guardians of the home, the pantry, the lineage. Romans made daily offerings to them at small shrines built into the walls of their homes. They gave wine, food, or simple gestures of smoke as acts of respect and maintenance. Petitioning wasn't dramatic, it was intimate. Spirit communication happened in the midst of ordinary life.

This intimacy is mirrored in Shinto practice in Japan, where people honor *kami* (spirits or deities) at public shrines and private altars. These nature spirits may dwell in trees, rivers, or stones. Communication is often subtle: a bow, bell, or whispered word. Shinto doesn't treat spirits as separate from nature but intrinsic to it. Petitioning a *kami* might involve an offering of rice or sake, and the purpose isn't to bargain, but to harmonize with the spirit's presence and role. In this way, the petition is an act of alignment, not control.

In modern spirit work, particularly in Western esoteric traditions, an unfortunate tendency is to treat spirit contact as a performance, a flashy act of "proof" or a demand for validation. But relationship doesn't thrive in performance. It thrives in consistency. This understanding is deeply ingrained in many folk magic traditions. Spirits aren't there to be impressed or tested, they're relational intelligences. If you want spirits to listen, you show up. You speak with honesty. You listen when there's silence. You learn their rhythms, their responses, and their symbols.

Spirit relationship also involves an awareness of energetic hierarchy. Some spirits function as protectors, while others are messengers. Some are ancestors who walk closely with us, while others belong to lineages or traditions we may only be touching from the outside. It is not appropriate to summon or demand the presence of a being who has not chosen to work with you. Consent matters on both sides of the veil.

Stories from Central and South American traditions tell of spirits withdrawing their presence from a household or community when they're not honored. In certain Andean belief systems, travelers offer *apus* (mountain spirits) coca leaves, songs, and intentions before crossing their domain. If the *apu* is disrespected or neglected, illness or misfortune might follow. This is not out of punishment, but because the natural balance has been disrupted. Relationship is a living current; when ignored, it recedes.

In modern animist and neopagan circles, this understanding of reciprocity continues. Many practitioners create spaces for listening as well as asking. Petitioning becomes a dialogue. Some spirits might respond through dreams, synchronicities, or changes in the emotional atmosphere. Others might appear in divinatory systems or through a felt sense, a weight in the air, a sudden knowing, or a presence that shifts the space.

In my own practice, a spirit may show me an image in words or sensations. An ancestral guide may not give an immediate resolution to a petition, but shift the path so new information becomes available. You don't always get what you ask for in spirit relationships. But you often receive what you need, if you're paying attention.

Trust – the foundation of connection

At the root of relationship-building and connection is trust. A petition made in desperation may still be heard. But a spirit with whom you've cultivated mutual respect over time is more likely to respond. Some call this energetic law; others call it grace. Either way, spirit responds to your sincerity and the clarity of your energetic presence.

It bears repeating: relationship is not a transaction. You're not creating a debt or engaging in manipulation. You are entering into an alliance built on presence, respect, and recognition. Petition thus becomes a language of shared intent, spoken across dimensions.

This work is not about mastering control. It's about entering into a living relationship with something greater than yourself. You aren't commanding spirits but communicating with them. Sometimes that means holding space for mystery. And sometimes that means walking away from the altar without answers.

The foundation of all true connection in spirit work is relationship, and like all relationships, it must be reciprocal. It requires your time, presence, honesty, and patience. Some spirits respond to ritual, others to silence. Some need offerings, others require only your awareness. The key is learning what each relationship needs and letting it develop naturally.

Trust in your own process. You may second-guess a message or doubt an encounter. That's normal. But with consistent practice, your clarity sharpens. You begin to recognize the difference between fear and intuition, between imagination and inspiration. The more you honor those quiet moments of connection, the stronger they become.

Connection is not a fixed state. It moves, stretches, and transforms as you grow. What once felt unreachable may later feel like second nature, and what once resonated may fall away entirely. This is the nature of spirit work; it mirrors your own evolution.

Connection also thrives in authenticity. Regardless of what tools you use or traditions you follow, when you come to spirit with reverence and openness, you'll be met in kind. The more time you spend in conscious relationship with spirit, the more natural it becomes to sense their presence in ritual and ordinary life. Trust that you're not making it up. Trust your gut. Trust the bond you're cultivating, even if you can't trace where the thread leads. It's okay to doubt. It's okay to question. But don't let skepticism harden into disconnection. Spirit responds to consistency and sincerity far more than perfection.

I've learned that spirits don't demand that we become something we're not, they meet us where we are. And when we approach with humility, honesty, and a willingness to listen, they tend to show up in ways that shift everything. Over time, the relationship becomes less about technique and more about presence. It's about becoming someone the spirits trust too.

Remember, your energy is your calling card. It precedes your words. It sets the tone of your practice. If your intention is clear and your heart is open, that's enough. You don't have to prove yourself. You just have to be willing to show up, again and again, in devotion and integrity. You're not earning connection, you're remembering it. You are not separate from spirit. You are learning to hear them again, and remembering more of who you are.

SUMMARY

- Petitions are intentional requests made to spirits with clarity and respect.
- Spirit relationships should be reciprocal, not one-sided.
- Building rapport with spirits involves patience, trust, and consistency.
- Offerings and gratitude are part of maintaining that relationship.

CHAPTER 11

Divination as dialogue

In its truest form, divination is not about predicting the future but deepening the conversation between the seen and unseen worlds. It's the act of listening with more than your ears, of feeling for a thread of meaning running just beneath the surface of things. At its heart, divination is relational. It offers reflection, direction, and insight; sometimes it brings clarity and other times a mirror that reveals what we already know but haven't admitted to ourselves.

Human beings have been looking for signs – in the sky, bones, the flight of birds, the shuffle of cards – for as long as we've known there is more to this world than what our hands can touch. In ancient Mesopotamia, priests read the livers of sacrificed animals to interpret the will of the gods. In ancient Greece, the Oracle at Delphi spoke cryptic prophecies while in a trance, surrounded by smoke and sacred stone. In precolonial African societies, trained diviners threw cowrie shells or bones to receive messages from ancestors and spirits. While the methods differ, the core impulse is the same: to commune, seek wisdom, and understand the hidden pattern.

Of course, these systems weren't just curiosities, they were deeply integrated into the cultures, spiritual worldview, and rhythm of life of those who practiced them. A diviner was more than a fortune teller; they were a mediator between human need and divine will. They were trusted to speak on behalf of spirit and offer guidance grounded in something larger than personal bias.

Spiritual literacy

In my own practice, I've come to think of divination as a kind of spiritual literacy. It's how we learn to recognize spirit's language. Not everything shows up in a lightning bolt or booming voice. Often, the message comes through a quiet image on a card, a sudden internal "click," a shiver when your finger lands on the right rune. Divination sharpens the inner ear. It trains us to notice.

Divination also demands humility. One of the greatest missteps in modern divination circles is assuming the tools do the work for us. That the deck, the pendulum, or the board itself is magical. But the truth is that the tool is only as clear as the channel using it. The cards don't speak, we speak through them. The runes don't decide, we interpret. There is always a filter: us.

This is why our relationship with our tools, intuition, and guides is so essential. Rather than seeking quick answers or convenient truths, divination is about entering into a dialogue with spirit and asking the right questions. And just like any other relationship, that dialogue deepens over time, with patience, trust, and consistency.

Sometimes people ask how I "know" the message is real. My answer is generally the same: because I feel it in my body. There's a difference between guessing and receiving. A real message vibrates, resonates, sticks. Over time, you learn to tell the difference between the static of your own mind and the signal of something deeper.

Not all divination systems are universal; some are deeply tied to a particular lineage, culture, or spiritual authority. For instance, Ifá divination within Yoruba traditions is a sacred practice, passed through initiation and training. It's not something you can casually borrow. The same is true of certain

Indigenous methods of reading signs, bones, or smoke.

A sacred practice

Divination is not something to take lightly. It is a sacred practice that deserves reverence. Whether you work with tools that are culturally familiar or personally significant, you should do so with integrity, listen more than you speak, research as much as you receive, and remain in right relationship with the work. The goal is never to claim power, but to cocreate insight. Divination is a bridge between realms, not a shortcut to control.

In my own spiritual development, divination was one of the first ways I truly felt spirit speak. Before I had names for guides or clearly established channels, I had cards. Those cards became a reflection of what I wasn't yet ready to hear directly. I had moments of uncanny accuracy that felt like a jolt to the chest. Other times the reading made no sense until days later when it suddenly did. That is part of the mystery of divination: it doesn't always answer in the way we expect. But if we're patient, it answers in the way we need.

Long before modern metaphysical stores and online tarot readers, divination existed at the heart of spiritual life. It was not entertainment or a quirky side-practice. It was a core means of receiving guidance, making decisions, and understanding the movements of fate, spirit, and the unseen world.

In ancient Mesopotamia, diviners read the entrails of sacrificed animals, interpreting patterns in the liver or lungs as direct messages from the gods. These practices, known as extispicy, were codified and respected; diviners were often consulted before battles or royal decrees.

Similarly in ancient China, diviners heated oracle bones until they cracked, then interpreted the fissures as signs. These markings would later evolve into early forms of Chinese characters, literally embedding divination into the language itself.

In ancient Greece, the Oracle of Delphi was not a mystic recluse, she was an institution. The Pythia, or high priestess of Apollo, spoke in trance and ecstasy, and temple priests recorded and interpreted her utterances. Kings and generals would travel for days to receive her wisdom.

Though the times have changed, the essential drive remains: people seek divination when they are at a crossroads, when they are uncertain but open.

Beyond Western traditions, we find rich and complex traditions: Ifá in the Yoruba religion uses sacred texts and numerical systems of interpretation; Kao Cim in Chinese temples uses numbered sticks shaken from bamboo canisters to divine a written oracle; and Tibetan Mo divination uses dice, astrological calculations, and ritual to seek the will of enlightened beings. These systems are often embedded within a broader cosmology, meaning that divination isn't just a practice, it's an expression of an entire worldview.

MY OWN DIVINATION PRACTICE

Early on, I was fascinated by the consistency of certain archetypes across systems. The Tower card in tarot, for example, bears a strange echo of the Norse myth of Ragnarok, or the biblical fall of Babylon. The more I read, the more I realized humans have always searched for signs, and the spirit world has always found ways to respond, whether through fire, smoke, bones, cards, or dreams.

What matters most in divination is the clarity of the relationship. I've used mass-produced and modestly illustrated decks and still received answers that pierced me to my core. I've also seen people with ornate, rare tools fumble to make meaning because their intention wasn't clear. Remember, not all spirits respond to all tools, and not all spirits should be consulted through divination. Part of building a spiritual practice is knowing when to ask, when to listen, and when to simply be with the mystery. Sometimes silence is the message.

Tools for divination

Divination tools are often approached with a kind of mystical glamour, but their real power is in the layered relationship among the diviner, the tool, and the unseen world. When I first picked up a tarot deck, I didn't feel lightning course through my veins or spirits flood the room. I felt curiosity. A quiet pull. And over time, through use, reverence, and honest questioning, the deck began to speak back.

Tarot has become one of the best-known divination tools in the West, though its origin is far less esoteric than many believe. The earliest decks appeared in fifteenth-century Europe as playing cards, with suits and court cards similar to modern playing decks. Centuries later, mystics and occultists, particularly those in the Hermetic and Theosophical movements, layered tarot with esoteric meanings drawn from astrology, Kabbalah, numerology, and alchemy. What began as a game became a map of the human soul and its dance with the invisible.

Pendulums have been used across traditions and timelines for their simplicity and directness. A weight on a string becomes a translator for subtle energies, responding to questions, sensing energy fields, or indicating direction. I've used pendulums in moments of deep uncertainty, when the conscious mind was too clouded to know what it truly wanted. Sometimes the swing of the pendulum didn't confirm what I wanted to hear, but it resonated with what I needed to see.

Though often associated with Norse traditions, runes offer their own form of dialogue. Carved into wood or stone, these symbols are more than letters of an ancient alphabet, they are storied archetypes including Fehu, the rune of wealth and beginnings, and Hagalaz, the rune of disruption and cleansing. Each pull is a conversation, not a verdict.

Beyond the tools themselves, the true depth of divination comes from the sacred art of interpretation. No card or rune or pendulum swing exists in a vacuum. It lives within the context, the moment, the question, the energy of the space. Two people might pull the same card and receive completely different messages because spirit is not static. It is alive, adaptive, and deeply personal.

I've had sessions where the same symbol appeared over and over in the cards, in a dream, then later in a conversation with a stranger. These patterns aren't a coincidence. They're communication. Spirit is often patient, but persistent. It will speak through whatever means are available, and divination offers a channel or formalized way to listen.

Lessons and boundaries

When practiced with humility, reverence, and patience, divination goes beyond being a method for receiving answers to become a pathway to deeper trust in the language of the unseen, the rhythms that pulse beneath surface reality.

As the veil between seen and unseen thins through repeated use of divinatory practices, it becomes important to establish boundaries, not just with spirits but with ourselves, others, and the work itself. Divination is not a parlor trick or a replacement for critical thought or therapeutic support. It is a sacred dialogue. And like all sacred things, it requires discernment and care.

One of the earliest lessons I learned, which I return to often, is never read for someone who hasn't asked.

Even if you have the best intentions, offering unsolicited insight crosses energetic lines. Consent is vital. You should always enter into spirit communication – whether with the divine, with guides, or through symbolic tools – with clear intent and mutual agreement. Reading for others is not about proving what you "know" or demonstrating your intuitive skill, it's about being in service, which requires a humility that honors both the person and the process.

Another boundary involves the temptation of overuse. When you first begin to receive accurate, insightful responses through divination, it can be tempting to go to the cards or the pendulum for everything. But divination isn't meant to replace your personal agency or deep inner knowing. Constant divination often clouds, rather than clarifies. Spirit can become quiet, or the messages may grow contradictory or vague, because your own energy is frayed or seeking certainty where none can exist. I've had to learn when to stop asking, when to sit with the discomfort of not knowing, and when to trust the unfolding of the path ahead.

Likewise, divination has limits to what it can, and should, answer. Questions about health diagnoses, legal matters, or outcomes involving other people's autonomy can quickly veer into unethical territory. You should never use divination to control others or as a bypass for difficult decisions. If the energy around a reading feels heavy, intrusive, or unclear, that's often a cue to pause, recenter, and perhaps return later, or not at all.

The final boundary is energetic hygiene. Divination is more than a mental or emotional process, it opens subtle channels. I have developed a practice of opening and closing every session with intention. I thank the tools, clear them, and close the energetic space, even when I'm working alone. This helps keep the messages clean and prevents lingering energetic residue. Without this, readings can feel muddled or exhausting, or even attract interference from non-benevolent energies.

Divination, at its core, is about learning to listen. Not just to spirit, but to yourself. Not just to signs, but to silence. And in a world so noisy with opinions, data, and distraction, that's a sacred act in itself.

SUMMARY

- Divination is a method for dialogue with spirits, not just a prediction tool.
- It can help clarify spirit messages or confirm intuitive impressions.
- Your mindset and energy affect the accuracy of your readings.
- Divination is one of many tools for spiritual communication.

CHAPTER 12

Invocation versus evocation

Throughout this work, we've touched on many forms of spirit interaction, from sensing to petitioning, from interpreting symbols to building relationships with unseen allies. At this stage, it's important to understand two key spiritual mechanics: invocation and evocation. These are not interchangeable magical terms; they represent very different energetic orientations, rooted in historical ritual and personal spiritual experience. In my own journey, I've found both invocation and evocation to be valid, powerful tools, though I approach each with very different intention and preparation.

Invocation

The term "invocation" comes from the Latin *invocare*, meaning "to call in." It is an act of internal communion in which the practitioner invites a spiritual force, deity, guide, or archetype to merge with or speak through them. Invocation is about embodiment. It often includes ritualized gestures, spoken prayer, chanting, or trance-inducing states to allow that force to move inward and express itself from within the practitioner's own body or consciousness.

When I invoke, I prepare to step aside and allow another consciousness to move through me. This requires deep trust and clarity. I've experienced invocation as moments of ecstatic union, feeling a deeper, fuller version of myself unfold as I align with a force greater than my ego. It can be humbling, beautiful, and often surprising in what comes through.

Sometimes invocation happens spontaneously. A person in deep grief may feel overcome with the presence of their loved one who's passed, not as a memory but as a direct and visceral awareness. A healer may find words pouring from their mouth that feel foreign and yet deeply true, as though a wiser force were speaking through them. A dancer may slip into a trance during ritual movement, embodying a force they didn't consciously summon but that clearly wished to move through their body.

Evocation

In contrast, the term "evocation" comes from *evocare*, meaning *"to call forth."* It is the act of summoning a spirit or entity to appear outside of the self. This might be visualized in the space around the practitioner, at the edge of a circle, or within a sacred container such as a triangle or designated area. Evocation often involves commanding or requesting the presence of a being, rather than inviting it to take residence within. It is more dialogic than participatory.

When I evoke, I set the space, call upon a spirit with reverence and boundaries, then engage in a kind of sacred conversation. I've evoked spirits for guidance, clarity, teaching, and protection during rituals. Sometimes I feel their presence subtly: a shift in temperature, a change in the air. Other times the energy becomes palpable, even electric. Still, the core of evocation is rooted in respect, not command. While some traditions speak of controlling spirits, I find that real power lies in mutual regard, not domination.

Evocation doesn't have to be dramatic or esoteric. Lighting a candle and calling on a benevolent spirit guide is an act of evocation. Whispering a prayer to a known ancestor and asking for their insight is evocation. Your interactions don't need to look like Renaissance spellwork or elaborate ritual; what matters is the conscious effort to reach across the veil and form a respectful, mutual exchange.

Distinct yet relational

The distinction between these two approaches is rooted in the ceremonial magical traditions of the West. In systems like the Hermetic Order of the Golden Dawn and Thelema, invocation is often used for divine or higher archetypal forces, angels, planetary intelligences, or divine names. Evocation is reserved for spirits, elementals, or what some systems would label "lower" entities, often those considered to dwell within the astral or sub-lunar planes.

But not all spiritual paths make this distinction so rigidly. In Afro-Caribbean traditions such as Santería and Vodou, possession by the spirits – often facilitated through music, rhythm, and communal ritual – can resemble invocation yet also include dialogue, healing, and teaching that one might associate with evocation. In many Indigenous traditions, spirit contact is not framed in such binary terms at all; the presence of ancestral or elemental spirits is experienced as both around and within, the lines blurring between self and spirit in ways that challenge the Western impulse to categorize.

This nuance between invocation and evocation will help you refine your own energetic awareness. Knowing when you are blending with spirit versus witnessing it externally can help maintain spiritual sovereignty and avoid confusion. I've worked with many who have opened themselves through invocation without understanding what they've invited in, only to find themselves overwhelmed, disoriented, or drained afterward. Likewise, attempting evocation without the proper grounding and shielding can leave you vulnerable to mischief, interference, or miscommunication.

Understanding this difference has shaped my practice in profound ways. It's not about one method being more advanced than the other, but about clarity of purpose and self-awareness. There are times to merge, and times to observe. Times to embody, and times to engage. The art of spiritual work lies in knowing which is being called for.

Ceremonies to invoke or evoke

In Western ceremonial traditions, particularly those influenced by Renaissance magic, Hermeticism, and grimoires such as *The Lesser Key of Solomon*, evocation is often associated with summoning spirits into physical appearance or interaction. These rites include lengthy preparatory rituals, complex sigils, sacred geometry, and strict protective measures. The magician is expected to be in full control of the spirit, with an emphasis on command, hierarchy, and ritual authority. These systems are deeply patriarchal and often influenced by Christian cosmology, where spirits are classified as angels or demons depending on their alignment with religious morality.

Contrast this with pagan and animistic traditions, in which the spirit world is not separate or adversarial but integrated with daily life. Spirits of the land, ancestors, animals, and elements are approached with respect and reciprocity. Whether one invites a presence inward or calls it to appear externally isn't often delineated, what matters is relationship. For example, in ancient Roman religion, people honored the household spirits (Lares and Penates) daily. They made offerings, not to control them but to maintain harmony between worlds.

In Hindu tantra and bhakti yoga traditions, invocation is a central part of devotional practice. Devotees don't simply imagine or symbolize deities, but call them into presence, sometimes internally through mantras and visualization, and other times externally into a *murti*, or icon. This isn't possession in the Western sense; rather, it's a merging of devotion and energy, where the practitioner aligns with divine presence to receive a *darshan* (sacred sight), blessing, or transformation. Invocation becomes a spiritual path in itself.

In Indigenous shamanic practices, there is often no clear boundary between invocation and evocation. A shaman might enter a trance and allow a spirit to speak through them (invocation), then journey to meet that same spirit in the otherworld to ask questions or seek healing (evocation). The method shifts depending on the need, the relationship, and the cosmology in which the work is being done.

Developing your practice

From my own experience working within a modern mystical framework, I approach both techniques with humility. The distinction between them is useful but not fixed. Sometimes what begins as evocation – calling a guide or ancestor into the room – becomes invocation when their energy floods the body or vision. Other times, I begin by inviting them inward but then find their wisdom is best perceived as a dialogue across space rather than from within.

An important layer is ethics and readiness. Invocation, in particular, requires discernment. Inviting a spirit to work through your body or consciousness is not something to do lightly. It's not a performance or party trick. Without solid boundaries and preparation, you can easily lose clarity, become energetically compromised, or mistake personal projections for divine guidance. You need to know not only whom you're invoking, but why. Are you seeking healing? Guidance? Expression? What are you offering in return? What do you consent to?

Likewise, you should never treat evocation as a form of domination. Spirits are not tools to be wielded; they are presences with autonomy, intelligence, and purpose. While some systems teach commanding spirits through names of power or ritual authority, my own path favors collaboration and reverence. Yes, you can summon a spirit, but will they answer? And if they do, how will they respond to your tone, your intention, your respect?

Modern mysticism has brought renewed interest in these concepts, often blended with psychological or archetypal frameworks. Some see invocation as the process of connecting with aspects of the higher self or divine mind, and view evocation as engaging with subconscious symbols or externalized aspects of the psyche. While this lens may lack the animistic richness of spirit traditions, it offers another valuable way to explore inner and outer mysteries, especially for those whose paths bridge the magical and psychological.

Invocation and evocation aren't just magical mechanics, but reflections of how we relate to the spirit world. Do we open ourselves fully and become a vessel? Do we call in allies to our space and share wisdom in sacred dialogue? Do we project inward or outward, above or below? These choices shape the ritual, the relationship, and the practitioner over time.

Ultimately, invocation and evocation are both modes of relationship: how we connect with unseen beings, forces, or consciousness beyond our ordinary sense of self. They aren't reserved for ceremonial magicians or mystics with decades of experience. They're natural, human ways of engaging the liminal, which have shown up in various expressions across cultures, spiritual paths, and personal callings.

With either method, your intention matters. Are you emotionally grounded? Are you in a place of centered presence, rather than desperation or fear? Have you researched the spirit or energy you're working with? Are you honoring its origin, its role, its nature? These are not gatekeeping questions, but invitations into responsibility.

A gradual unfolding

Beware of assuming too much, too soon. Energetic shifts aren't always signs of possession. Not every presence you feel is a spirit guide. The more we long for contact, the easier it is to project meaning onto every intuitive hit. This is where you need self-awareness. We must learn to ask: Is this a true presence? Or is it my mind, my memory, my desire?

Part of what builds strength in spirit work, especially when invoking or evoking, is repetition and relationship over time. A single interaction may be confusing or vague, but repeated consistent and respectful engagements begin to shape something meaningful. You come to know how a particular spirit feels, how their presence shifts your thoughts or energy, and how they communicate with you uniquely. You begin to discern their signature.

In my own journey, the most transformative connections have unfolded gradually. I've called on guides who didn't answer until the seventh or eighth attempt. When they finally did, the bond was unmistakable. I've also invoked presences that arrived quickly and intensely, only to realize later that I wasn't prepared to hold their energy. Both types of experiences have taught me to be patient, discerning, and humble. The more I've learned to listen, the more these relationships have deepened, not as tools, but as allies.

Whether you're drawn toward invocation or evocation (or both), allow yourself to move at your own pace. This isn't a competition or hierarchy of ability. Some people naturally resonate with inner communion, feeling the whisper of spirit within their own consciousness. Others feel more attuned to calling presences into the space around them, engaging through sensation, symbol, or dream. Both paths are valid. Both require care.

Remember, just because you can invite a spirit in, doesn't mean you should. Power alone isn't the goal here. This work is about relationship, not control. Just as you wouldn't let a stranger into your home without some sense of trust or purpose, the same is true for the spirit world. Ask questions. Set boundaries. Make offerings if your tradition supports it. Say thank you. Close the door when the work is done.

SUMMARY

Invocation and evocation are two expressions of a larger truth: the veil between worlds is permeable, and with care, intention, and humility, we can engage across that veil in ways that heal, illuminate, and transform. These practices are sacred, not because they require elaborate rituals or complex language, but because they remind us that we are never alone. We are in conversation, whether we realize it or not. And how we choose to speak, listen, and invite makes all the difference.

» Invocation invites a spirit into yourself or your space to connect, while evocation calls a spirit to appear externally without merging energies.

» The choice between the two depends on intention, safety, and the type of spirit.

» Knowing the distinction is critical for responsible and effective spirit work, and how you engage shapes the entire experience.

Annotated bibliography
(further reading)

Abel, C. "The Duality, Paradox, and Harmony behind the YinYang." *Medium*, accessed May 20, 2020. https://medium.com/the-philosophers-stone/symbology-of-symbols-the-yinyang-7da94af198a6

This article supported exploration into dualistic spiritual frameworks, referencing the symbolic interplay of energy often encountered when discussing spirit realms and energetic balance.

Bell, Catherine. *Ritual: Perspectives and Dimensions.* Oxford University Press, 1997.

Bell's foundational work on ritual helped frame key discussions around ceremonial structure, including invocation and evocation, grounding practices, and memory encoding through repeated spiritual acts.

Boyd, Robert, and Peter J. Richerson. *Culture and the Evolutionary Process.* University of Chicago Press, 1985.

This text informed broader anthropological perspectives on how spiritual practices evolve within cultures, aiding discussion on collective memory, psychic development, and transmission of tradition.

Colosimo, Natalie. "Elementals and Earth Spirits." *The Psychic School,* accessed October 20, 2021. https://psychicschool.com/elementals-and-earth-spirits/

Colosimo's explanation of elemental energies informed descriptions of spirit types, particularly nature spirits and animistic forces across belief systems.

Connerton, Paul. *How Societies Remember.* Cambridge University Press, 1989.

This book supported analysis of embodied memory and how physical or psychic rituals reinforce spiritual knowledge across time and generations.

Durkheim, Émile. *The Elementary Forms of Religious Life.* Translated by Karen E. Fields. Free Press, 1995.

Durkheim's foundational sociology provided historical context for the social function of spiritual belief and its connection to group identity, especially when exploring mediumship and divination.

Halbwachs, Maurice. *On Collective Memory.* Edited, translated, and with an introduction by Lewis A. Coser. University of Chicago Press, 1992.

This classic text on memory studies offered a grounding theory for how communities preserve spiritual beliefs and experiences across time, including ancestral veneration.

Harari, Yuval Noah. *Sapiens: A Brief History of Humankind.* Harper, 2015.

Referenced to provide context on the cognitive evolution of humanity's belief in unseen realities and the development of ritual and myth as meaning-making systems.

Harper, Douglas. "Etymology of demon." *Online Etymology Dictionary,* accessed November 19, 2021. https://www.etymonline.com/search?q=demon

Used to trace the linguistic and cultural history of the word "demon," clarifying common misconceptions and providing nuance to modern interpretations in spirit work.

Illes, Judika. *Encyclopedia of Spirits.* HarperCollins, 2009.

A cornerstone reference for spirit typologies, this encyclopedia was used throughout to support terminology and distinctions among spirit kinds, particularly when addressing historical figures and global lore.

Ingold, Tim. *The Perception of the Environment: Essays on Livelihood, Dwelling and Skill.* Routledge, 2000.

Ingold's ecological anthropology contributed to framing spirit communication within environmental and sensory-based interactions, especially regarding animism and land spirits.

Malinowski, Bronislaw. *Magic, Science and Religion and Other Essays.* Waveland Press, 1992.

This classic work provided historical grounding for the discussion of magical thinking and belief systems that underpin spirit work and psychic development.

Olick, Jeffrey K., Vered Vinitzky-Seroussi, and Daniel Levy. *The Collective Memory Reader.* Oxford University Press, 2011.

This compilation enriched the manuscript's theoretical framework for collective cultural memory in spiritual traditions and practices of invocation.

Snell, Daniel C., ed. *A Companion to the Ancient Near East.* Wiley-Blackwell, 2007.

Provided context on ancient Mesopotamian and Near Eastern spiritual systems, especially in tracing the origins of spirit hierarchy, possession, and ritual.

Soca, Gabriel. "What are Starseeds and How to Know if You Are One?" *Gaia*, accessed November 15, 2020. https://www.gaia.com/article/am-i-a-starseed-types-characteristics

This article supported modern spiritual identity archetypes and the evolving language of psychic self-conception.

Tilley, Christopher. *A Phenomenology of Landscape: Places, Paths and Monuments.* Berg Publishers, 1994.

Referenced when writing about sacred landscapes and the role of environment in spirit interaction and perception.

Weschcke, Carl L. "The Goal of High Magick Is Initiation." *Llewellyn Worldwide*, accessed February 12, 2020. https://www.llewellyn.com/encyclopedia/article/25576

Referenced in discussions around ceremonial magic, particularly the purpose of initiation and layered relationships with spirit beings.

Whitehouse, Harvey. *Modes of Religiosity: A Cognitive Theory of Religious Transmission.* AltaMira Press, 2004.

Provided a theoretical model for how spiritual knowledge is retained and transmitted through structured and spontaneous experiences across cultures.

About the author

Sirian Shadow is a versatile and multifaceted practitioner, psychic, and author who provides spiritual guidance for empowerment and transformation. His mission is to inspire wisdom and empower personal and spiritual truth. He is the author of the oracles *Shadow of Darkness* and *Earth and Bone.*

sirianshadow